SIGNALS AND SIGNAL-BOXES

OF GREAT BRITAIN

SIGNALS AND SIGNAL-BOXES
OF GREAT BRITAIN

DAVID HUCKNALL

SUTTON PUBLISHING

First published in the United Kingdom in 1998 by
Sutton Publishing Limited · Phoenix Mill
Thrupp · Stroud · Gloucestershire · GL5 2BU

British Library Cataloguing in Publication Data
A catalogue record for this book is available from the British Library

ISBN 0 7509 1322 3

TM ALAN SUTTON™ and SUTTON™ are the
trade marks of Sutton Publishing Limited

Typeset in 11/13 pt Bembo.
Typesetting and origination by
Sutton Publishing Limited.
Printed in Great Britain by
Butler & Tanner, Frome, Somerset.

CONTENTS

CONTENTS

FOREWORD

TIM GUEST, Bsc, PhD, CEng, MIM. CPhys, MInstP
CHAIRMAN, SIGNALLING RECORD SOCIETY

In comparison with the moving elements of the railway scene – locomotives and rolling stock – signalling came comparatively late to the notice of railway enthusiasts. Although dedicated individuals were at work before the Second World War, interest only began to take off in the 1960s, when so much of the system was being lost to the closures of the Beeching era. Although signalling still remains something of a specialism among enthusiasts, the growth of the Signalling Record Society from 6 members in 1969 to around 600 in 1997 is indicative of the growth of interest in this area.

What began to be realised, just in time, was that there were few areas of railway operation where more in the way of pre-grouping, let alone pre-nationalization equipment and working practices, had been retained. In addition, at many locations, on lines being closed, little or nothing in the way of change had taken place since they were first signalled seventy or eighty years before. For that matter, this was often true for many places on the busier lines which were being retained.

Think of the then Southern Region where similar Sykes Lock and Block instruments were operated in two quite different ways on the Central (former LBSC) and South-Western (former LSWR) divisions. Or spare a thought for signalmen working on the parallel former GWR and MR lines between Gloucester and Standish Junction. They worked the GW lines with GW instruments, the Midland with Midland instruments and while keeping two train registers, laid out in different styles, operated GWR rules on the GW lines and LMS on the Midland lines. Joint railways were often a fruitful hunting ground for signal-boxes, complete with curious mixtures of indoor and outdoor equipment from the constituent companies.

For many signalling enthusiasts, interest began by collecting copies of signal-box diagrams, the stylized charts of the track and signals hung over the levers. Indeed, the Society began in 1969 largely as a correspondence club of diagram collectors. Signal-boxes were, in theory, closed to the public so that it was that much harder to get first-hand knowledge of their contents and what went on inside. However, our present-day knowledge is the better both for the many signalmen and their supervisors who turned a blind eye to amateur visitors and also for interested professional signal engineers who were able to save historic material from the wastebin and bonfire.

Later on, interests developed, more systematic research became possible. Evidence was collected on the ground and in national and local archives which, together with the sale of railway drawings from Collector's Corner, meant that signalling enthusiasts were able to build up knowledge in more specialist areas.

FOREWORD

It became possible to work out details of the development of signalling and track layouts at particular places throughout their history. Nevertheless, there remain locations where we know exactly what was there in 1890 but not in 1970.

Specialist interests such as signal-box architecture, lever frames and block signalling instruments, have also developed to give a detailed picture of 'box equipment. For some reason, the signals themselves still seem to be somewhat neglected.

While the larger pre-grouping companies were usually responsible for the design and installation of their signalling equipment, many others employed one or other of the specialist signalling contractors whose characteristic designs could be found on lines throughout the country.

As a result of the various railway modernization plans, panel signal-boxes controlling many miles of line became the standard on most main lines. It should be remembered that many of these installations are well past their intended working life. More recent developments have led to the introduction of computer-controlled interlockings with the signalmen viewing the monitor screens. Recording is still required though it may now be necessary to preserve the computer software in order to see how the system worked!

Among signalling devotees there has often been something of a conflict between those enthusiasts who devote themselves to detailed technical studies and other who relish the atmosphere of former days. To the latter the former seemed obsessed with cold technical detail at the expense of appreciating the working environment and skill of the signalmen themselves. In this book the author has tried to show something of both approaches to the subject in a way which I hope will be of interest to the general railway enthusiast as well as the signalling specialist.

INTRODUCTION

For years, I watched and photographed trains in various parts of Britain, paying scant attention to the signals and the signal-boxes that controlled their movements. They were just part of the general railway scene and I assumed they would always be there. Therefore I largely ignored them. For example, as a teenager I spent many hours sitting on the fence by the side of the East Coast main line at Ranskill, unaware that only a couple of hundred metres away stood a signal-box built on behalf of the Great Northern Railway in 1875. I also made several visits to the 'box near Parkgate and Aldwarke station but only because it provided an excellent vantage point for trainspotting.

To come across a signal-box now can seem a notable event. Without the activity and general clutter that once characterized the railway scene, one can see clearly what odd and fascinating structures many of them are. Many retain, both internally and externally, equipment and characteristics of railway companies which ceased to exist some seventy-five years ago or more. They are a fragile link with our railway history.

The growth of railway traffic in the nineteenth century had led to the provision of a vast number of signal-boxes to control stations, sidings, junctions and level-crossings. Even in the late 1950s/early 1960s, particularly in the vicinity of important stations, it was not unusual to have several 'boxes separated by quite short distances (see Tables 1 and 2). For example, between Reading and Kidlington, there were twenty-eight of which Oxford itself had eight. The decline in the number of signal-boxes and the disappearance of semaphore signalling started gradually but accelerated dramatically. When this is quantified, its increasing rapidity becomes obvious. The Introduction to *The Signal-Box* (1986) points out that, 'In the heyday of mechanical signalling around the turn of the century, some 13,000 'boxes were in current use and the total number of 'boxes ever built was something like double this number'. The Introduction continues, 'Now, there are only 2,000 left, and they are disappearing at a rate of a hundred or more each year'. Six years on *The Signal-Box Directory* for 1992 states in the Preface, 'In the five years, 1.1.1987–31.12.1991, 370 BR 'boxes have been abolished and only 20 new ones opened'. The number of British Rail cabins still existing on the 1 January 1992 was 1,198. The situation on 1 January 1997 was that some 1,078 'boxes remained on Railtrack of which 895 were Block Post signal-boxes (Kay, 1997).

Alterations in track layout and signalling improvements have always taken place on Britain's railways and such improvements have always meant change. At Manchester London Road station, for example, the controlling railway companies (the Great Central Railway and the LNWR) had introduced the earliest form of power signalling in Britain in 1909. The GCR's system was electro-pneumatic while the LNWR had an all-electric system controlling semaphores. Fifty years

Table 1: Signal-boxes: Reading West to Kidlington (1960)

SIGNAL-BOX	DISTANCE BETWEEN SIGNAL-BOXES	
	miles	yards
Reading West		
Southcote Junction	–	–
Oxford Road Junction	1	44
Reading General		
Main Line East	–	–
Main Line West	–	770
West Goods	–	946
West Junction	–	1,430
Scours Lane Junction	–	1,254
Tilehurst Station	–	1,408
Pangbourne Station	2	1,584
Goring and Streatley		
Station	3	374
Cholsey and Moulsford		
Station	3	1,474
Didcot		
Moreton Cutting	3	88
East Junction	1	638
West End	–	748
Foxhall Junction	–	726
West End	–	–
North	–	946
Culham		
Appleford Crossing	–	1,540
Station	1	1,012
Radley		
Station	2	330
Sandford	1	528
Oxford		
Kennington Junction	1	572
Hinksey South	–	1,254
Hinksey North	1	198
Station South	–	836
Station North	–	396
North Junction	–	550
Wolvercot Siding	1	1,166
Wolvercot Junction	–	1,408
Kidlington Station	2	1,738

Table 2: Signal-boxes: Waterloo Station to Farnborough via the Main Line (1960)

SIGNAL-BOX	DISTANCE BETWEEN SIGNAL-BOXES	
	miles	yards
Waterloo Station	–	–
Loco Junction (Vauxhall)	1	1,689
Queen's Road (Vauxhall)	–	1,059
Clapham Junction		
West London Junction	–	706
'A'	–	1,056
Earlsfield Station	1	1,319
Wimbledon		
'A'	1	1,079
'B'	–	560
'C'	–	660
Raynes Park Station	–	1,269
New Malden Station	1	536
Surbiton		
Station	2	697
Hampton Court Junction	1	167
Esher		
East	–	1,425
West	–	559
Walton-on-Thames		
Station	2	1,213
Oatlands	–	1,699
Weybridge		
Station	1	262
Byfleet Junction	–	1,730
(from Addlestone Junction)	–	1,538
West Byfleet Station	1	850
Brookwood Station	3	1,060
Farnborough		
Sturt Lane Junction	4	333
(from Frimley Junction)	–	248
Station	1	162

later, signal engineering works in connection with the first stage of the electrification of the Euston–Manchester/Liverpool lines resulted in the closure of twenty-seven manual signal-boxes between Crewe and Manchester via Styal. The new power signal-box at Manchester Piccadilly meant that eleven signal-boxes were abolished and two were downgraded to shunting frames. A total of 848 signal levers from the original 1909 scheme were involved. The entire Manchester–Crewe line was signalled by just three power signal-boxes.

It was in the 1950s and 1960s that the pace of change began to accelerate. For example, a new power-operated 'box was built at Euston, just outside the station. It opened on 5 October 1952. It was necessary because the signalling system dating from 1905 was difficult to operate. Three of the station's 'boxes (Euston no. 1, no. 2 and no. 3) were replaced and colour-light signalling and continuous track circuits were installed.

At about the same time, the central section of the Southern Region of British Railways was resignalled. The first stage, between Bricklayer's Arms Junction and Norwood Junction, was brought into use in October 1950. The second stage, from Streatham Common to Selhurst and from Battersea Park to Streatham Common, was inaugurated two years later. Eleven manually-operated 'boxes were replaced by three power-operated ones – Clapham Junction B, Balham and Streatham Junction.

By 1963, the opening of Nuneaton power signal-box marked the completion of the first half of the resignalling of the London Midland main line from Liverpool/Manchester to Euston via the Trent Valley. Further south, significant changes were also occurring. The opening, in 1964, of signal-box at Watford Junction meant the replacement of ten mechanical 'boxes (Harrow no. 1, Hatch End, Bushey, Watford no. 1, Watford no. 2, King's Langley, Boxmoor, Berkhamsted, Tring no. 1, Tring no. 2). Signal-boxes at Watford Tunnel North End, Bourne End, and Northchurch and Tring Cuttings, had already closed.

Although the foregoing paragraphs have concentrated on the West Coast main line, a similar process was being repeated throughout the country. April 1959 saw the commissioning of the route-relay interlocking signal-box at Newcastle Central station which controlled 10 miles of line including Manors station and the High Level and King Edward Bridges. Four signal-boxes (totalling 538 levers and 34 switches) were replaced. The PSB at Gateshead, opened in 1963, took over the work previously done by five cabins (Bensham Curve, King Edward Bridge, Greensfield, High Street and Park Lane): 12 miles of track were involved. The following year, Heaton's PSB completed an 84-mile stretch of colour-light signalling and track circuiting between Durham and Burnmouth.

After the rather piecemeal resignalling of the West Coast main line, the 1970s saw work begin on the East Coast. Approval for the King's Cross–Sandy section of the ECML was given in late 1970 and, by early 1972, the scheme was extended as far north as Doncaster. The Doncaster–King's Cross route was to be controlled by just three power 'boxes at King's Cross, Peterborough and Doncaster. In December 1972, Peterborough power 'box was commissioned. Initially, it controlled just the station area up to Crescent Junction cabin to the south of the station, but this was then extended to Werrington in the north and Fletton in the south. By April 1973, it became responsible for 13 miles of the ECML route between Holme and Helpston. By 1977, the Peterborough 'box was fully operational.

Approval for the Doncaster scheme was obtained in 1974 for an 84-mile stretch from milepost 101 to milepost 185. It was expected to replace fifty-one mechanical signal-boxes with completion expected in 1977. Work was slow because of the complexity of the railway system in the Doncaster district, with its many junctions and routes, and it was not until July 1979 that the first stage was operational. By February 1980, however, its control area extended between milepost 100 (the south end of Stoke Tunnel) to milepost 163 on the down line and milepost 169 (just south of Temple Hirst Junction) in the up direction. The scheme replaced fifty-two mechanical signal-boxes and eleven gate-boxes.

In the 1990s, changes have been relentless. Following the publication of the Government's White Paper, 'New opportunities for the Railways' in 1992, the Railways Act was passed some eighteen months later. Under this Act, Railtrack was created to supervise railway operations and infrastructure. Within this organization the Major Projects Division planned further resignalling work. Schemes included the Cardiff Valleys resignalling and, during 1994, the closure of all remaining mechanical signal-boxes throughout Airedale and Wharfedale. Railtrack's London North Eastern division is now working on 'Project EROS' (Efficiency by the Rationalization of Signal-boxes), a signalling modernization programme which, although it will take place in five phases over ten years, will decimate that region's remaining 'boxes.

One cannot help but regret the passing of signalling methods and equipment that have served us so well for decades but modernization must take place if the railways are to limit the advance of the most heavily subsidized industry in the country – road transport.

It has been a pleasure to gather material for this book and, as it progressed, so my enthusiasm for the subject grew. I have been delighted to find so many examples of the signalling work of the pre-Grouping railway companies or their contractors - the neat little wooden cabins of the Midland Railway, the Saxby and Farmer 'boxes of the LBSCR, painted green and cream or light blue and white, with their ornamental eaves and upper lights. Even later structures have their appeal – the Southern Railway's 'Odeon' 'boxes still suggest, as they must have done over sixty years ago, '. . . an excitement, a verve, a gusto for something different . . .' to quote George Behrend. Without exception, the 'boxes I have visited have been incredibly well kept inside and the signalmen and other Railtrack employees still maintain a pride in their work and their links with the past. An account I came across recently sums this up. It concerns a visit to the 'box at Walnut Tree Junction by the Monmouthshire Railway Society. 'Comment was made by our Railtrack host on the fine GWR block instruments as opposed to the Bakelite-bodied versions found on the Midland. . . . It was remarkable to see that to this day some old Company rivalry still surfaces.'

This book does not cover any specific area or company exhaustively or attempt in any great depth to discuss signal-box architecture. It is simply a reflection of places and objects that have taken my fancy, from a rusting bucket on the rear wall of a 'box in South Wales to the sheer size of the LNWR's Stockport no. 2 signal-box.

WESTERN REGION

The pre-1958 Western Region of British Railways coincided closely with the boundaries of the pre-Grouping Great Western Railway. The GWR was one of the best signalled lines in the country. From 1859, it had a signal works at Reading but even in the 1860s and 1870s only part of its signalling work was carried out 'in house', the remainder still went to contractors. From April 1885, however, the Reading signal works was meeting all the Company's needs.

The earliest signal-box design from Reading appeared between 1869 and about 1875. According to an accepted classification system (*The Signal-Box*, 1986), this is categorized as the GWR Type 1. The Type 2 design was used around 1876–80 but very few examples remain. The 'box at Par in Cornwall is one such structure. The design that is probably most associated with the GWR is the Type 7. It was introduced in 1896 and many examples are still in use. Brick built, with a hipped roof and large eaves bracket, they have 'three up, two down' windows and the characteristic 'torpedo' ventilators on the roof ridge. The overall effect is one of pleasing solidity and reassuring attention to detail.

In the 1960s, the former Western Region began to decimate its mechanical signal-boxes, particularly on its lines out of Bristol and London. For example, apart from the poor old 'box at Puxton and Worle, there are no signal-boxes on the present Railtrack system between Bristol and Exeter. Similarly, the only 'boxes between Exeter and Paddington are at Westbury, Reading and Slough. In spite of this, a few areas still remain where the traditional 'boxes are the rule rather than the exception. These include Cornwall (the line between Penzance and Liskeard), the Kidderminster–Worcester–Malvern area and, until recently, parts of South Wales. The former GWR/LNWR Joint Line through Abergavenny and Hereford to Shrewsbury and the Shrewsbury–Oxley line are further examples.

At various times over the years, there have been plans to resignal Cornwall. Although the number of 'boxes has been steadily reduced, rail traffic there remains regulated by the signal-boxes. Some are close to, or even over, a hundred years old. St Erth, for example, was opened in 1899. Truro dates from the same year while Par and Lostwithiel were brought into service in about 1879 and 1893 respectively. The present Penzance 'box is a mere sixty years old.

In the South Midlands in 1960, there were twenty-nine signal-boxes from Birmingham Snow Hill to Droitwich Spa. Snow Hill South (an early power 'box) closed in 1960, three further closures occurred in the mid- to late 1960s and thirteen were taken out of service in the 1970s (the majority in 1972/3). Now only four remain. They are, nevertheless, fascinating. Hartlebury is the last surviving example of a McKenzie and Holland Type 2 'box. Droitwich Spa signal-box is one of the fine Type 7 'boxes. Opened in 1907 with a 79-lever GW frame, it retains an impressively long frame.

Particularly in Wales, the Great Western was associated with several quasi-independent companies such as the Cambrian, the Taff Vale and the Barry Railways. Only the Taff Vale has been included in the present book. The threatened Walnut Tree 'box and almost inaccessible Radyr Quarry Junction are fine examples of the TVR and its signalling contractors.

The Great Western Railway identified its signal-boxes precisely. Names such as Box Signal Box have amused past railway writers. Whereas some other regions replaced the pre-Grouping nameboards, quite a few former Western Region signal boxes still carry their original cast-iron names. Stourbridge Junction 'box remains Stourbridge Junction Middle Signal Box and Blakedown retains its original identification as Churchill & Blakedown Signal Box although the 'Churchill &' has been painted out. Many Western Region 'boxes still retain a cast-iron notice on their doors whereby the Great Western Railway warns the public not to enter its signal boxes.

The lower quadrant signal with its characteristic finial remains to this day a reminder of the GWR. Although colour-light signalling is used extensively throughout the system, many impressive examples remain. The six-arm bracket signal at Radyr is now the largest former Western Region signal existing on Railtrack. At the north end of Worcester Shrub Hill station, the bracket signal carrying the semaphores controlling the Down lines makes a colourful and impressive display. At St Erth, seen against the background of the signal-box, the bracket signals seem still to be waiting the arrival of a 'Grange' from Penzance or a 45XX Prairie tank engine from St Ives.

(*Opposite, bottom*) The signal-box at St Erth and one of its lower quadrant semaphore signals. The 'box, a GWR Type 5, was opened in 1899. It has a 69-lever Great Western VT3 frame dating from 1929. A few years ago, on a similar sunny afternoon, I was invited into the 'box by the signalman. The spotless floor shone in the sunlight. The levers were coloured blue, red, white, black and yellow, all with gleaming, polished handles. At that moment I felt that Cornwall's railway history was still appreciated here.

In 1964, there were seventy signal-boxes controlling the railways in Cornwall. Now, from St Germans to Penzance, a distance of 70 miles and 6 chains, the main line is controlled by only eight and St Erth controls a section working to Penzance in the west and Roskear Junction in the east.

August 1996 David Hucknall

The signal-box at Penzance is the largest surviving 'box in Cornwall. Situated between the railway and the A30, it lies under the shadow of the wall from which, over the years, countless people must have looked down on trains approaching and leaving the station. It faces south-east, across Mount's Bay towards St Michael's Mount and beyond. A GWR-style structure, classified as a Type 12B, it was built on the site of the old railway shed and opened on 24 April 1938. Here, an ubiquitous HST passes it on its way to Paddington.

The signal-box works with the 'box at St Erth in the east and controls the station area, the sidings and the depot at Ponsandane, working colour-light signals from its 75-lever GW VT5 frame. Many years before there were signal-boxes close by, at Long Rock and Ponsandane, which controlled movements to and from the locoshed at Long Rock and the carriage sidings. Ponsandane 'box was flat-roofed because the local influential Bolitho family would not tolerate the view of Mount's Bay from Chyandour House being spoiled.

9 August 1996 David Hucknall

St Erth station is the junction for the 4½-mile branch to St Ives. It has been described by A. Bennett (1988, p. 33) as an 'Imposing, spacious junction station' with Up and Down platforms serving the main line and a bay on the up side for the branch line.

In this photograph, the left-hand bracket signal at the eastern end of the Up platform gives the road to a Penzance to Plymouth train. The left-hand post (or 'doll') on the signal controls the Up main to branch connection. In the distance, St Erth signal-box can be seen. Beyond the fence, on the left-hand side of the picture, the starter signal for trains on the St Ives branch is 'off'.

10 August 1992 David Hucknall

The window in the door to the signal-box at St Erth reflects a typical Cornish sky.
David Hucknall

GREAT WESTERN RAILWAY
NOTICE
NO UNAUTHORIZED PERSON ALLOWED IN THIS BOX
BY ORDER

Trains entering Truro station from the east cross the Carvedras viaduct over the rivers Allen and Kenwin. Coming off the viaduct, a unit that will form the 11.48 to Penzance is seen passing Truro signal-box.

The signal in front of the road crossing is Truro's Up main start signal. Truro signal-box, a GWR Type 1a of 1899, has altered little over the years although the station layout has. Formerly Truro East 'box, the present structure survived the closure of the West 'box in November 1965. It even had its lever frame replaced in 1971 with one from Bristol East Depot main line signal-box (*Signal-Box Directory*, 1992).

1 August 1991 David Hucknall

The Up starter signal is off and 'Warship' class locomotive no. D864 *Zambesi* begins to move out of Truro station with the 12.00 to Bradford. Until late 1971, Truro had several sidings to the north and the west of the station and some of the lines led to the engine shed. Beyond the locomotive is an old, narrow type of backing signal on a wooden post, used to control shunting movements which might involve brief occupation of the main line.

12 July 1965 David Hucknall

The signal-box at Lostwithiel (Lostwithiel Crossing) controls a section of the Cornish main line and is one of only six level-crossings between Plymouth and Penzance. It also oversees china clay traffic on the branch to Fowey Docks. It works absolute block with Par in the west and track circuit block with Liskeard 'box in the east.

The great age of Lostwithiel 'box – 101 years old – was all too apparent when this photograph was taken. A GWR Type 5, with a brick base and a timber top, it has a pleasant, gabled porch and some of the tallest roof finials I have seen.

August 1994 David Hucknall

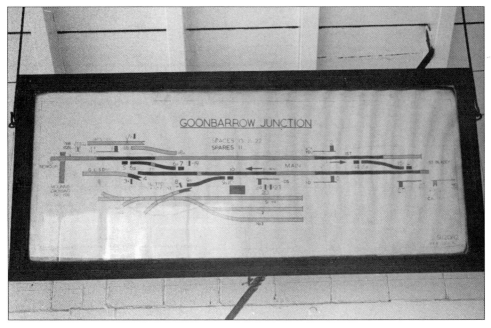

The inside of Goonbarrow Junction signal-box. It shows the schematic diagram identifying the points and signals operated by levers with the corresponding number. The 'box controls not only movements into the clay works but traffic on the single line to Newquay.

January 1996 Lawrence James

Goonbarrow Junction signal-box is on the Par–Newquay line. It is 1½ miles from Luxulyan in the direction of Bugle (6¼ miles from Par).

The gradient is 1 in 40 up the valley to Luxulyan and the 1½ miles to Goonbarrow Junction is at 1 in 67. At Goonbarrow, the line used to diverge to the left as the last branch built by the CMR – the 3½-mile single line to Carbean sidings.

Here the signal-box at Goonbarrow (GWR Type 7d of 1909) can be seen, together with some of the sidings and signals it controls. A detailed diagram of the tracks and signalling can be seen elsewhere. Over the years, the fortunes of the china clay industry have fluctuated and during the 1960s many mineral branches closed. The Goonbarrow branch closed in 1965, leaving only local sidings.

January 1996 Lawrence James

OXFORD, WORCESTER AND WOLVERHAMPTON

Seventeen miles from Oxford on the former Oxford, Worcester and Wolverhampton Railway lies Ascott-under-Wychwood station. The line from Wolvercot Junction on the GWR to Evesham was opened by the OW&W on 4 June 1853. According to *Pearson's Railway Rides – Cotswolds and Malverns*, 'The complex history of the OW&W Railway belongs not so much in the annals of railway enthusiasm as in the casebooks of legal precedent and financial fraud'.

A level-crossing on a minor road between the B4437 and the A361 separates the single platform at Ascott from the signal-box. The inner door of the 1883 signal-box still carries the GWR warning against unauthorized entry.

1 January 1996 David Hucknall

7

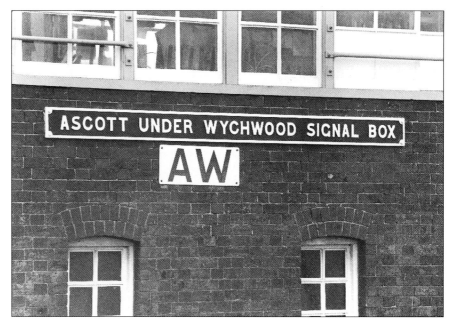

Nameboards on signal-boxes varied from company to company. Methods commonly used included cast-iron letters screwed directly on to the timberwork and cast-iron letters screwed onto a timber board (*The Signal-Box*, The Signalling Study Group, 1986).

Between the 1890s and the 1940s, cast-iron name-plates with the letters and plate cast in one piece were standard on the GWR. The lengthy name-plate of Ascott under Wychwood Signal Box (probably a later addition as the 'box dates from 1883) can be clearly seen.

During 1944, various issues of *The Railway Magazine* carried occasional notes on the 'compendious titles carried by GWR signal-boxes'. Pride of place possibly went to 'Quakers Yard West Tunnel Junction Signal Box', the name-plate of which extended the entire length of the 'box front with about 3 inches to spare at each end (*The Railway Magazine*, 90 (550), p. 117, March/April 1944). This was probably closely followed by 'Cheltenham Spa Malvern Road East Signal Box' (*Railway Magazine*, 90 (551), p. 185, May/June 1944).

1 January 1996 David Hucknall

The former Great Western line between Oxford and Evesham follows the Evenlode Valley through Kingham past Adlestrop to Moreton-in-Marsh, situated on level ground about 400 feet above sea level. Moreton-in-Marsh station was under a light covering of snow in this photograph; the signal-box, opened in 1883, was not in use and the station was deserted apart from a woman in the booking office.

5 January 1997 David Hucknall

A side elevation of (Churchill &) Blakedown signal-box. The reference to Churchill, although painted out, is clearly visible on the nameboard. The 'box is classified as a Type 4c, built by the Great Western Railway in 1888. It incorporates a gable-end porch, complete with toilet. It was one of the first designs to which the GWR added roof finials.

12 January 1997 David Hucknall

The well-kept signal-box at Blakedown stands out against the dark conifers in this pleasant, semi-rural corner of Worcestershire. Blakedown lies on the former OW&W line south of Stourbridge Junction, approximately midway between there and Kidderminster.

12 January 1997 David Hucknall

Stourbridge Junction Middle signal-box, opened in 1901, is now the sole survivor of four 'boxes which once controlled activities in and around Stourbridge Junction. In addition to the Middle signal-box, the 'boxes were Stourbridge Junction North, Stourbridge Junction South and Engine Shed Sidings (C.R. Potts. *An Historical Survey of Selected GW Stations*, vol. 4, Oxford Publishing Co., 1985, p. 152). The first 'box to be closed was Engine Shed Sidings in May 1969. On 30 December 1973, the South 'box (seventy-four levers) was closed. The North 'box, with sixty-nine levers, was the next to go. It closed on 29 July 1978 when a colour-light signalling scheme, operated from the Middle signal-box, was introduced.

8 July 1996 David Hucknall

The nameboard on Stourbridge Junction Middle signal-box. The abbreviation 'Jc' for Junction is one of several variations to be found throughout the country.

8 July 1996 David Hucknall

An unusual bracket signal with centrally-pivoted arms stands at the end of the Down platform at Droitwich Spa station. The lower signal is the Down main to Down loop intermediate home signal.

2 April 1996 David Hucknall

The signal-box at Droitwich Spa stands high on an embankment that takes the railway over the Droitwich canal via a brick bridge. The 'box is a former GWR Type 7d structure of 79 levers. This splendid cabin has the hipped roof typical of the Type 7s and the wide areas of glass at operating floor level can also be seen.

2 April 1996 David Hucknall

Droitwich Spa station was opened in February 1852 simply as Droitwich, by the Oxford, Worcester and Wolverhampton Railway (the 'Old Worse and Worse').

Clearly seen in this photograph is the fork in the line north of the station. The left-hand branch is the OWW route between Worcester and Wolverhampton, while the right-hand branch leads to Stoke Works and Birmingham. In the fork stands Droitwich Spa's fine signal-box.

David Hucknall

Hartlebury station is on the line between Kidderminster and Worcester. It was on the Oxford, Worcester and Wolverhampton Railway and was also the terminus of the GWR's Severn Valley branch which ran for 39½ miles to Shrewsbury.

Hartlebury Station Box, as it was known, was opened in 1876. It is the last surviving example of a Mackenzie and Holland Type 2. Once fitted with a 30-lever frame, it became a panel 'box, 'Hartlebury', in 1982. It works under AB regulations to Droitwich Spa.

23 April 1996 David Hucknall

Although the station at Henley-in-Arden on the North Warwickshire line is unmanned and more than a little down at heel, it still retains a pleasant atmosphere. Although built relatively late in railway history (it opened for passengers on 1 July 1908), the line provided an important route from the Midlands to the south and west. It was on the route followed by 'The Cornishman' which ran between Wolverhampton and Penzance.

The signal-box at Henley-in-Arden dates from the opening of the line. It is a Type 7d 'box built by the Great Western Railway and opened in 1907. A fine brick-built structure, it has large 'three up, two down' windows and the usual cast-iron name-plate.

16 March 1997 David Hucknall

Shirley is on the former Birmingham and North Warwickshire line between Tyseley and Bearley North Junction. The signal-box at Shirley is situated on the Down platform of the station which over the years has won various best kept station awards. The 'box is a GWR Type 7d with 31 levers. It works absolute block with Henley-in-Arden and TCB with Tyseley No. 1 signal-box.

20 April 1997 David Hucknall

The former Aylestone Hill signal-box (renamed simply 'Hereford' in 1973) dates from 1884 and is on the Shrewsbury–Hereford line. The contract for resignalling work at Hereford was awarded to the Railway Signalling Co. of Liverpool. It is classified as a 'Wellington'-type cabin because it is in the style of the four new signal-boxes erected at Wellington station during the resignalling there. Hereford 'box is basically a Saxby Type 1 structure (R.D. Foster. *A Pictorial Record of LNWR Signalling*, OPC, Oxford, 1982, p. 235). It was initially fitted with a Saxby rocker frame but this was replaced in 1938 with a Great Western-type four-inch-centres frame with vertical Tappet locking. A panel was installed in 1984.

7 July 1994 David Hucknall

The Shrewsbury–Hereford line was an important LNWR/GWR joint venture, linking two significant rail centres. Leominster lay on the route and as a town of some consequence had a station reflecting its status. An outstanding feature was the large signal-box which stood high above the platform, supported on columns and horizontal girders. At the southern end of the station was another signal-box, originally built to oversee the level-crossing for the Worcester road, the South End 'box.

Now only the South End signal-box remains, in spite of the fact that the level-crossing was removed when an overbridge for the road was built. An interesting, all-brick 'box, dating from 1875, it is almost square in plan (15 ft 2 ins by 15 ft 1 in) and similar to the Saxby and Farmer Type 1 cabins found on the northern sections of the LNWR. Fitted in 1901 with an LNW tumbler frame, it had a GW VT5B installed in July 1941.

It is now named just 'Leominster'. A distinctive metal pinnacle which once surmounted the hipped roof has long been removed.

October 1996 David Hucknall

Moreton-on-Lugg was the first station out of Hereford (Barr's Court) on the Shrewsbury and Hereford line. In the early 1950s, North-and-West expresses using this route might be hauled by a Bristol 'King' class 4–6–0. On the level track past Moreton, they would hurry by, touching about 60 m.p.h., before slowing for the climb to Dinmore.

The station at Moreton is now closed and only one- and two-coach units, carrying a few passengers, drift by. It is difficult to find a suitable vantage point from which to photograph this signal-box and this shot was taken from the remains of the platform. It shows the former Great Western Railway Type 12a 'box, opened in 1943. This replaced an older structure which had been at the opposite side of the crossing.

October 1996 David Hucknall

SOUTH OF WORCESTER

The entrance to the signal-box at Ledbury station.
October 1996 David Hucknall

A Great Western train from the direction of Malvern comes off the branch line and enters the north end of Worcester Shrub Hill station on the Up main line. It will later form a train to Paddington. Dominating the scene is the bracket signal which controls that part of the station. Reading from left to right, the arms are Down main to branch starting, Down main advanced starting to locoshed and Down main advanced starting.

To the right of the bracket signal is that for the Up main to (Down) Up main starting and the Up main to branch starting (R. Czaja. *Mechanical Signalling in Worcestershire*, Part 1, The Signalling Record, no. 59, p. 154, Sept/Oct 1996).

28 May 1997 David Hucknall

The present Pontypridd Junction signal-box is significantly altered from the structure that was opened in about 1907 by the Taff Vale Railway Co. at the time of the reconstruction of the passenger station. During the 'rationalization' of the rail facilities in the Welsh valleys during 1970, the operating floor of the 'box was drastically reduced in length at the station end. Evidence of this shortening is clearly visible.

23 March 1997 David Hucknall

Seen from the platform end, Pontypridd Junction signal-box surveys a railway system considerably changed since its opening in 1907. Pontypridd, which is situated at the confluence of the Taff and Rhondda rivers, was once referred to as the 'Grand Junction of the Western Valleys' (O.S. Nock. *British Railways in Action*, London, Nelson, 1956). Not only did it deal with coal traffic bound for Cardiff, Barry, Penarth and Newport, but it regularly handled 11,000 passengers a day at seven platform faces. The necessary working points and signals required 230 levers (D.S.M. Barrie. *A Regional History of the Railways of Great Britain*, vol. 12, South Wales, Newton Abbot, David & Charles, 1980).

Although totally deserted when this photograph was taken, Pontypridd station remains impressive. It is, however, slowly but surely decaying beneath its coating of dirt. The signal-box looks well cared for but the intricate bargeboards that would have adorned the gable-ends were replaced during the shortening of the 'box. The former Taff Vale Railway Company's main line leading to Abercynon crosses from left to right. The Rhondda line is not visible but runs away to the left towards Porth and Treherbert.

David Hucknall

The magnificent six-arm bracket signal that controls the junction dominates this photograph taken from the footbridge at Radyr station, looking towards the south-east. The left-hand lines, passing directly in front of Radyr Junction signal-box, curve away to Llandaff and Cardiff Queen Street. The lines veering sharply to the right head towards Radyr Quarry signal-box and Danescourt.

Apart from its size (it is probably the largest former Western Region signal remaining on Railtrack), it carries below it the no. 1 Siding Home signal, a rare mechanical route indicator.

23 March 1997 David Hucknall

A closer view of Radyr Junction signal-box. An anonymous-looking 'box, painted dark brown and merging into the background of leafless trees, it is an example of a British Railways' Western Region standard design.

Sometimes referred to as the 'plywood wonder', it was originally built in about 1958 at Swindon Station East: it was never commissioned. The 'box and frame were re-erected at Radyr Junction, opening in June 1961. It replaced a Taff Vale Railway 'box located a little nearer Llandaff.

23 March 1997 David Hucknall

Radyr Quarry Junction signal-box is extremely difficult to find. The approach is via the old access road to the former Radyr locoshed. This potholed rocky track passes under the disused Llandaff North to Radyr Quarry railway spur. Eventually, on the left, the 'box can be seen across the rusting railway lines of the former Radyr Yard, now rapidly disappearing under encroaching buddleias.

The signal-box is an example of a Taff Vale Railway cabin. Opened in 1899, it has seen the calamitous decline in railway activities from the days when 7¼ million tons of coal a year were exported from Bute Docks alone. Radyr Quarry Junction 'box survives now to signal trains on the City Line to Cardiff.

23 March 1997 David Hucknall

The centrally pivoted Up main starting signal at the Pontypridd end of Taff's Well station is now a rare type. The post to the right is all that remains of the signal that controlled access to the Nantgarw branch.

13 November 1996 David Hucknall

An end elevation of the former Taff Vale Railway's signal-box at Walnut Tree Junction. The precise date of opening is apparently not known. It seems to have been between 1900 and 1922.

Built in the style of the McKenzie and Holland Type 3 'boxes for the TVR, the decorative bargeboards and large area of operating level glass are clearly seen here. Fitted with a 79-lever GW VT5 frame in 1951, only seven of the levers are now in use.

As a result of the introduction of the Radyr–Pontypridd resignalling during 1997, this 'box will be redundant. It seems likely, however, that it will be dismantled brick by brick and rebuilt in a heritage centre at Barry Island.

13 November 1996 David Hucknall

A view inside Abercynon 'box, looking towards the entrance, shows some of the levers, the Tyers token apparatus (no. 527) and one of the two control panels fitted. One such panel, installed in 1977, controlled the Stormstown Junction area about a mile south of Abercynon, where a branch diverged and crossed the River Taff on its way to Dowlais Cardiff Colliery.

David Hucknall

The fire bucket hanging on the rear wall of Abercynon signal-box.

13 November 1996 David Hucknall

Abercynon signal-box stands at the Pontypridd end of the platform at Abercynon South station. It is a second-hand GWR Type 27c, brought into use at the station in 1932. Its previous locations had been Birmingham Moor Street (1909) and Didcot Foxhall Junction (1915). The 'box windows appeared on GWR Type 7 'boxes to improve the signalman's view.

Two lines can be seen in this photograph. Both are single lines and serving Merthyr Tydfil (left-hand line) and Aberdare (the right-hand line). Trains stop at Abercynon 'box to receive tokens to work these lines.

13 November 1996 David Hucknall

Pencoed Crossing Ground Frame is a Great Western Railway Type 27C 'box, opened in about 1905. Pencoed stands approximately 187 miles from Paddington on the section of the South Wales main lines between Bridgend and Cardiff. The 'box is made of timber and has a hipped roof with distinctive eaves brackets. The operating floor windows, which can be seen indistinctly behind their wire mesh, are again 'three up, two down'.

Pencoed station was closed in late 1964, some 114 years after its opening. It was opened again in May 1992.

23 March 1997 David Hucknall

Tondu was once a major railway centre. From there lines ran north (up the Llynfi Valley to Maesteg), north-east (up the Ogmore (Ogwr) Valley), east to Llanhoran, south to Bridgend and south-west to Porthcawl. Tondu railway shed stood in the centre of a triangle of lines, with Ogmore Junction, Tondu station and Tondu North Junction at the corners.

Tondu station is rather forlorn now. Where once the railway bustled with life, little remains. Photographed from the bridge spanning the station, the former Middle signal-box surveys not the shed and its sidings or the routes to the Ogmore Valley and to Llanhoran, but the under-used tracks of a much truncated system. Tondu signal-box dates from 1884.

March 1997 David Hucknall

The former Tondu Middle signal-box seen from the platform end. Opened in 1884, the 'box began life as a GWR Type 3 but, in the past thirty-five years, its appearance has changed markedly. It once had four sets of locking-room windows which were removed when the 'box was rebricked. The operating floor windows which once consisted of four by three pane glazed sections are now the more functional 'three up, two down' type. A chimney which once protruded from the rear of the roof has also been removed.

March 1997 David Hucknall

EASTERN REGION

In England, the constituent companies of the LNER included the Great Northern, the Great Central and the Great Eastern Railways. On 1 January 1948, the Eastern Region of British Railways was formed from the former southern area of the LNER, but it also included lines such as the one-time Metropolitan/GCR joint line from Aylesbury to Verney Junction. Over the next few years, some adjustments were made to regional boundaries but a more significant change resulted from the 1953 Transport Act whereby the management of the Eastern Region reverted to divisions, and the names Great Northern lines and Great Eastern lines re-emerged.

The pre-Grouping companies that had initially formed the southern part of the LNER served a very large area. The GER covered Essex, Sussex, Norfolk and parts of Cambridgeshire. Jointly with the GNR, it was also involved in the line from Huntingdon to March, Lincoln, Gainsborough and Doncaster. The GNR ran from King's Cross to the north via Peterborough, Grantham, Retford, Doncaster, Selby and York. It also served Bradford and Leeds. Further south, it had secondary routes from Grantham to Boston and Skegness and to Nottingham, from Peterborough to north Norfolk and from Hitchin to Cambridge. The boundary between the GNR and the GER was, approximately, the East Coast main line. The Great Central or, as it was known prior to 1897, the Manchester, Sheffield and Lincolnshire Railway, established itself on both sides of the Pennines. The MSLR had acquired the Great Grimsby and Sheffield Junction Railways' main line and its Lincoln branch, so its influence extended from north Lincolnshire to Manchester and beyond. The GCR also served the Yorkshire, Derbyshire and Nottinghamshire coalfields. Through its extension from Annesley to Quainton Road, the GCR provided a fast link between Manchester, Sheffield and Marylebone. Unlike the North Eastern Railway with its domination of Northumberland, County Durham and North Yorkshire, no territory belonged exclusively to the GCR. It competed with the GNR in Lincolnshire, with the GNR, the Midland, the LNWR and the L&YR in the old West Riding of Yorkshire. Even with its extension, it only reached London over lines shared with the GWR and Metropolitan Railway.

Presently, the old Eastern Region comes administratively under the control of two Railtrack zones. The East Anglia zone serves a region almost identical to that of the GER. The remainder is dealt with predominantly by the London North Eastern zone.

Returning to the former GNR lines, the 1955 Modernization Plan for Britain's railways promised, in the Eastern Region, electrification and track widening from King's Cross to Leeds and possibly York. In the end, it took over twenty years to achieve this. During this time, the ECML operated through areas controlled by mechanical signal-boxes supported by intermediate colour-light signals installed in the 1930s. Although the plan had long been to control the whole of the ECML in Eastern Region territory, by just three 'boxes, Peterborough was only commissioned in spring 1973. Traditional signal-boxes such as Essendine North, Sandy, Greatford and Crescent Junction continued to function as coverage from Peterborough 'box which was gradually extended. Peterborough power 'box was eventually linked to King's Cross in December 1977.

Away from the main line, the former GNR lines, particularly in Lincolnshire, remain largely signalled by the absolute block method. With the exception of two relatively short sections, the line between Peterborough and Doncaster is worked by this technique as far as Beckingham in the northbound direction. Similarly, the route between Nottingham, Sleaford, Boston and Skegness is AB signalled except for the Sleaford East–Heckington and Hubbert's Bridge–Sibsey sections.

Of the existing former GNR 'boxes, many were erected during the period between 1870 and 1890. Classified as Type 1 (*The Signal-Box*, 1986), examples can be found at Ranskill, Rauceby, Ancaster, Sleaford, Eastfield and St James Deeping to mention a few examples. Usually with steeply-pitched roofs and large finials, they tend to have characteristic highly-decorated bargeboards.

The old MSLR had routes that stretched from Grimsby and Cleethorpes, across the Yorkshire coalfield to Woodhead, Manchester and beyond. The MSLR/Great Central 'wove a cat's cradle of competitive lines' (Fiennes, 1967) with the Midland between Barnsley and Annesley, both striving to obtain lucrative coal and steel traffic. In 1960, some 115 signal-boxes controlled the Manchester (London Road)–Grimsby line. About this time, British Railways began to curtail activities drastically on the former GCR lines. In 1965, for example, a significant number of Sheffield–Manchester trains were diverted from the Woodhead route to the Hope Valley line. By 1969, through train services were withdrawn. The route closed completely on 21 July 1981. Large and lonely, its former MSLR Huddersfield Junction 'box is a reminder of what might have been, at present, an exceedingly important route.

Although only twenty-six 'boxes now control the remaining ninety-three miles of the Manchester–Grimsby route, clusters of the MSLR's signal-boxes remain. Between Brancliffe East Junction (a GCR 'box) and Retford Thrumpton, four out of six 'boxes originate with the MSLR. On the lines between Gainsborough and Immingham, five are from the MSLR. The remainder (Wrawby Junction, Barnetby East, Brocklesby Junction) were built by the GCR. Many of the later GCR 'boxes opened on lines serving the coalfields of the North Midlands have either disappeared or are under threat. Only a few examples of the final GCR signal-box design (the Type 5), still exist. Outside Lincolnshire, the remaining ones are at Maltby Colliery, Welbeck Colliery Junction and Clipstone West.

On the former GER lines, there are areas where the world of semaphore signals and pre-Grouping signal-boxes remains. On the line from Norwich to Lowestoft/Yarmouth, for example, there are 'boxes at Whitlingham Junction, Brundall, Cantley, Reedham (two), Somerleyton swing-bridge, Oulton Broad station and Lowestoft. The Ely–Norwich line has nine, including Shippea Hill, Lakenheath, Brandon, Thetford and Harling Road. In contrast, on the main line between Norwich and Liverpool Street, only the 'box at Trowse swing-bridge and the gate-box at Stowmarket remain, between Norwich and Colchester. Prior to 1989, there were fourteen signal-boxes between Colchester and Liverpool Street including Marks Tey, Witham, Chelmsford, Ingatestone, Shenfield, Gidea Park, Romford and Goodmayes. Since the opening of the Liverpool Street IECC in 1989, the number of 'boxes has gradually declined. Of the eight currently standing, several are out of use and four will have been demolished by the time this book has been published.

This chapter has taken a very brief look at the 'boxes on the former GER lines. The main line is represented by Marks Tey, Chelmsford and Ingatestone. Of these, Marks Tey, is due to be closed and demolished and although Chelmsford 'box is already closed, it will be preserved where it stands. On the secondary routes, the signal-boxes examined include a couple around Ely and a similar number on the Cambridge–Bury St Edmunds line.

Finally, of the semaphore signals remaining in the Eastern Region, all are restricted to the LNER/British Railways upper quadrant type. The last pre-Grouping signals I saw on the Eastern Region were an ex-GNR somersault signal at Retford and a former GCR distance near Braithwell. That was back in 1963. The very last of the pre-Grouping signals on the region were to be found on the Skegness branch. Examples of Edward French's somersault signal developed for the GNR after the Abbot's Ripton disaster, they certainly lasted well into the 1980s and I have recently been told that they may still be there.

Lawrence James on duty as a telegraph lad inside Crescent Junction signal-box in September 1961. The 'box was located at the southern end of Peterborough North Station and controlled train movement there.

The duties of a telegraph lad included maintenance of the train register. This involved recording the bell signals passed between the 'boxes on either side of the relevant signal-box. He also informed other signalmen along the line of order and times of trains passing Peterborough in the Up (King's Cross) direction. For this he used either the telephone or the telegraph single needle instrument.

In this photograph, the young Mr James is ringing the Goods Line Block bell to Fletton Junction. This was *not* part of a telegraph lad's usual duty.

Lawrence James

FORMER GREAT NORTHERN RAILWAY LINES

KING'S CROSS–DONCASTER–LEEDS

The signal-boxes at Essendine North and South were situated on the East Coast main line between Grantham and Peterborough. The 'box shown in the photograph is Essendine North. Brick-built, probably between 1905 and 1915, it has all the features of a former GNR Type 4a 'box but it lacked finials and the bargeboards were plainly decorated when compared to some GNR 'boxes further south. Essendine, together with many others, closed during the mid-1970s with the introduction of Peterborough power signal-box.

Lawrence James

Sandy is on the East Coast main line approximately 44 miles from King's Cross. The 'box was on a relatively level stretch of track (rising at 1 in 766 towards Tempsford).

Sandy signal-box was situated to the south of the station on the down side of the ECML. It was classified as a Great Northern Railway Type 1 'box but did not have the elaborate bargeboards typical of that design. The vertical boarding at the gable-ends and the curved tops to the window frames were, however, typical. The 'box was removed during the last phase of colour-light installation on the line in the mid-1970s.

Lawrence James

This photograph shows the signal-box at Three Counties, about 3½ miles north of Hitchin on the East Coast main line. Here, in the Up direction, the gradient is 1 in 400 before the long 1 in 200 climb to Stevenage. At this point, a superb cast-iron bridge spanned the four tracks of the main line. Part of this can be seen near the 'box. Before the resignalling of the ECML, Three Counties 'box worked with Hitchin Cambridge Junction to the south and Arlesey to the north.

Three Counties 'box had all the characteristics of a GNR Type 3 structure – no finials, narrow plain bargeboards and operating floor and locking-room windows, four and two panes deep respectively. The vertical boarding with battening was also typical.

Lawrence James

Connington North signal-box was built in 1942/3 in conjunction with the Connington marshalling yard which was intended to provide an alternative for the many freight trains using the New England yard. Built in the 'ARP' (Air Raid Precaution) style, the 'box has a concrete roof and a substantial brick base. Such 'boxes were not designed to survive direct hits by bombs but rather to minimize the effects of blast and debris.

During the early 1950s, Connington North signal-box was winched on rollers, moved a hundred or so metres to the north and placed on a new base so it could operate the level-crossing gates shown in the photograph.

Lawrence James

Greatford signal-box on the East Coast main line was removed during the resignalling of the 1970s. Approximately 10 miles north of Peterborough, it worked with Tallington 'box to the south and either Essendine North or South cabins, depending whether Essendine South was closed or not to the north. It was also responsible for the level-crossing where a minor road between Greatford village, Belmesthorpe and Stamford crossed the line. Greatford had a combination of some GNR features – tall finials, highly decorative bargeboards – but the roof has an atypical shallow pitch.

Lawrence James

'A3' class 4–6–2 no. 60106 *Flying Fox* passes Doncaster South signal-box on its approach to the station. Doncaster South was opened in January 1949 and was one of seven signal-boxes which controlled the station area until resignalling in the late 1970s. The other 'boxes were Marshgate, 'C' box, Doncaster North, St James' Junction, Bridge Junction and Sand Bank.

The resignalling work taking place in 1948 was implicated in the Balby Bridge disaster of 9 August 1948 in which eighteen passengers died.

May 1964 David Hucknall

The signal-box at Ranskill (144 miles from King's Cross on the East Coast main line) was opened by the Great Northern Railway in 1875. It controls the crossing on the minor road between the villages of Lound and Torworth. Comparison between this photograph, taken in November 1995, and one taken from almost the same spot and published in *The Railway Magazine* of October 1940 shows how, externally, relatively little has changed. The intervening fifty-odd years have seen the removal of the balcony that ran at window level around the front of the 'box and the brick chimney at the back. Apart from this, everything, even the location and style of the nameboard, seems the same. Inside, however, considerable modifications have been made; a panel was fitted in 1975, replacing the frame and levers.

David Hucknall

Class J50 0–6–0T no. 68988 of Copley Hill shed passes under a signal gantry shortly after leaving Leeds Central Station with empty stock for Copley Hill sidings. Seen from Holbeck High Level station, the signal-box to the left-hand side of the gantry support is Leeds Central 'B' 'box which was situated where the curve from Geldard came in.

In the background, to the left of the 'B' 'box, stands the Wellington Street South goods depot which was formerly known as the High Level goods depot until 1951.

25 April 1962 David Holmes

The station and signal-box at Ancaster, on the line between Barkston East Junction and Sleaford, stand on ground slightly higher than the village. The approach to the station is along a rising potholed road leading from Ermine Street (B6403). The signal-box is immediately visible, standing starkly against the sky to the west of the station.

Opened in about 1880 this former GNR 'box is fitted with a Saxby and Farmer frame, having 30 levers, installed in 1887. Ancaster signal-box is still very attractive. It has a steeply pitched roof and tall finials. What had once been highly decorative ridge tiles are now looking the worse for wear, but this is compensated for by the elaborate bargeboards which are a feature of the signal-boxes along this line.

8 July 1996 David Hucknall

Sleaford West signal-box oversees a level-crossing on a relatively minor road. The gates are of traditional appearance.

Sleaford became part of Britain's railway system on 16 June 1857 when an 11-mile-long branch from the Great Northern main line near Barkston brought the Boston, Sleaford and Midland Counties Railway to the town. The BS&MCR was absorbed by the GNR on 1 January 1865.

Sleaford West 'box is a former GNR Type 1, apparently dating from 1880 (*The Signal-Box Directory*, 1992) but there is uncertainty about this. The former GNR 'boxes of the 1870s to 1880s, however, 'defy all attempts at categorization'.

28 May 1995 David Hucknall

Heckington station is on the line between Sleaford and Boston. The signal-box, which is at the end of the Sleaford-bound platform, is said to be a former Great Northern Railway Type 1 of about 1877 (*The Signal-Box Directory*, 1992). Dominating the station and the 'box is Heckington windmill.

Just in front of the level-crossing gate is an upper quadrant starting signal mounted on a concrete post. This is noteworthy because it is a very early example of the use of concrete in signal engineering. Shortages of timber at the end of the First World War led both the GNR and the Great Central Railway to use the material.

28 May 1995 David Hucknall

(*Opposite, top*) In the 1880s, the local authorities and other interested parties around Boston paid for the construction of a dock. The Great Northern Railway built a branch line to serve that dock but, much to the annoyance of the investors, would not contribute to its costs although it would greatly benefit from the rail traffic generated.

Here can be seen the signal-box, the crossing gate and, beyond that, the dock. The 'box was built to control the traffic on the dock branch and also regulate its crossing of London Road. It is an octagonal structure and once had a 12-lever Saxby and Farmer frame. The dock branch is now closed but the 'box survives, its windows boarded up. Even as late as 1996, the former GNR somersault signal still stands, although its spectacle glasses are broken.

21 August 1985 David Holmes

King's Cross–Cambridge

Foxton station is on the line between Cambridge and King's Cross via Hitchin. The Hitchin–Cambridge line has a long and varied history. The Eastern Counties Railway (later absorbed by the GER) opened the original line from Shepreth Branch Junction to Shepreth on 25 April 1851. The Royston and Hitchin Railway (and its extension to Shepreth) was worked by the GNR and was opened on 25 August 1851. Foxton was about 1½ miles into the Great Eastern section from Shepreth.

This photograph shows the 1878 GNR 'box at Foxton. It oversees the point where the railway, just west of the station, is crossed by the A10, Cambridge–Royston road.

September 1995 David Hucknall

L1 class 2–6–4T no. 67787 approaches Radcliffe-on-Trent at 2.12 p.m. with the 1.36 p.m. Grantham–Nottingham Victoria train.

The origins of the railway at Radcliffe-on-Trent lay with the Ambergate, Nottingham and Boston and Eastern Junction Railway which opened the first part of the line from Nottingham to Grantham on 15 July 1850. Within two years (19 May 1852), a meeting approved the purchase of the AN&B&EJR by the Great Northern Railway. From April 1855, the GNR took over all rolling stock and other effects on a 999-year lease.

The influence of the GNR can clearly be seen with the somersault signals which dominate this shot. Although the signalposts are made of concrete in this case, there were examples of lattice posts in the vicinity of Radcliffe. With regard to the locomotives used on the line, local traffic during the 1950s and early 1960s was dealt with by class B1 4–6–0s, J6 0–6–0s, B12/3 4–6–0s and L1 2–6–4Ts.

14 March 1962 David Holmes

FORMER GREAT EASTERN RAILWAY LINES

LIVERPOOL STREET–COLCHESTER

Ingatestone is a pleasant town that is served by the former Great Eastern Railway's Liverpool Street–Norwich line. Just over 23 miles from Liverpool Street, it is on a short, level stretch of track between Shenfield (20.2 miles) and Chelmsford (29.7 miles).

The signal-box at Ingatestone is a former GE Type 7 of 1905. It overlooks the point where Station Lane crosses the main line. As a height gauge, traffic passes under a line with small bells attached. The spotlight to illuminate the crossing shines brightly.

In the recent (October 1996) resignalling of the Shenfield–Hatfield Peverel section of the GE line, Ingatestone 'box has been reduced in status. It is now a gate-box controlling the Station Lane crossing and the Church Lane LC by closed circuit television.

27 September 1994 David Hucknall

Chelmsford signal-box is now deserted. It was closed in October 1996 during the resignalling of the Shenfield–Hatfield Peverel section of the former Great Eastern Railway's line to East Anglia. Unusually, it stands on the station buildings and the veranda once provided the signalmen with an excellent view of railway activities. A former Great Eastern Railway Type 7 structure of 1899, it was obviously significantly modified to suit its location.

March 1997 David Hucknall

Now heavily buttressed, the signal-box at Marks Tey is in a poor state of repair. The paintwork is flaking and the window frames are rotting. Formerly named 'Marks Tey Yard', the 'box is a Great Eastern Railway Type 7 of the 1890s and retains most of the features shown in the official drawing for all-timber 'boxes of this design (*The Signal-Box*, 1986). The working level windows are in three pane by three pane sections; the locking-room windows are five panes across by two panes deep. The bargeboards are moulded and beaded. The eaves retain the louvres hung on pivots described in the drawing. The gallery and balcony are supported on wrought iron brackets.

Marks Tey 'box was extended in the 1920s but subsequently reduced in size. The once extensive sidings opposite the cabin have now been removed while the land between the 'box and the road to the station is rented out.

March 1997 David Hucknall

The massive supports holding Marks Tey signal-box in place can be seen in this photograph taken from the Norwich end of the station platform.

The station, 46 miles and 49 chains from Liverpool Street, is on the main line to Colchester and Norwich. Marks Tey is also the junction for a branch that runs to Sudbury in Suffolk. The 'box stands by the side of the Down line and, years ago, a Down passenger loop ran behind the 'box with the Up goods loop behind that.

March 1997 David Hucknall

The Great Eastern Railway arrived at Sleaford on 6 March 1882 via the Great Northern/Great Eastern joint line that passed to the east of the town and a spur that connected the line to Sleaford station. By 1 August of the same year, the Lincoln–Sleaford–Spalding line became operational under the joint committee. Via the joint line, the GER had a route from East Anglia to the north and north-west of England and ran trains between Doncaster and Liverpool Street, and Lancashire and Harwich.

Sleaford North signal-box was opened by the Great Eastern Railway in 1882. Here the Type 2 wooden 'box and the level-crossing gates appear almost unchanged from the date of their opening. Only the essential Portaloo and power cables intrude.

28 May 1995 David Hucknall

A small road leads from the B1304 to the village of Dullingham and crosses the railway at Dullingham station. Now an unstaffed halt, the station is on the line between Cambridge, Newmarket and Bury St Edmunds. The signal-box stands on the Cambridge side platform and oversees the level-crossing. Two lines run through the station but one is a passing loop on the bi-directional line between Chippenham Junction and Cambridge.

Dullingham signal-box is, unusually, a Stevens-built Type 4 cabin of the former Great Eastern Railway. It was opened in 1884. It looks so reassuringly traditional and well cared for that it is surprising to find it contains not a lever frame, but a low table with a panel, monitor screen and keyboard. In the corner, however, a pot-bellied stove is still used. Apart from the hours between approximately 12.00 a.m. to 6.00 a.m., Dullingham 'box is open daily, working with Chippenham Junction and Cambridge 'boxes. The duty signalman was Mr Marsden, formerly of Chippenham Junction.

4 April 1997 David Hucknall

(*Opposite, bottom*) A view of Chippenham Junction from the window of the signal-box. The line to Dullingham leads away to the left. The centre track is designated the Down Bury line although it becomes the Up main at the junction. The line on the right is the Up Bury which then becomes the Down main.

The logbook of Chippenham Junction 'box records the opening and closing times of Dullingham signal-box and, in addition to the descriptions and times of passing trains, it records any unusual happenings. On Friday 23 December 1994, for example, Dullingham 'box closed at 12.05 a.m. and reopened at 5.30 a.m. At 16.33 on the same day, the Chippenham Junction signalman advised the yard at Bury St Edmunds that sparks were coming from a wagon wheel on train 4L39. The train was subsequently stopped at Bury, the fault corrected and the line declared clear and safe at 17.02.

David Hucknall

Chippenham Junction signal-box, near Newmarket, is isolated and also difficult to photograph. It stands at the top of a shallow cutting at a point where the Ely–Bury St Edmunds and Cambridge–Bury lines join. To reach the 'box, a sandy road through the trees on the Al-Bahathri gallops must be followed and one of the gallops crossed.

Reported to be a Great Eastern Railway Type 7 cabin opened in about 1925 (*The Signal-Box Directory*, 1992), it is small and contains an undated 16-lever McKenzie and Holland frame although one lever has been removed. A flat-roofed extension has been added at some time. Before this, work must have taken place in very cramped conditions.

Chippenham Junction is interesting from the point of view of railway operations. Three types of block signalling are practised. On the section to Kennett, the next 'box to the east, absolute block signalling is used. On the bi-directional line to Dullingham, tokenless block is used while on the line to Ely, track circuit block is in operation. There is an additional complication at Chippenham Junction. On the double track sections, the line description changes, the Up Bury line from Ely becoming the Down main to Kennett and vice versa.

4 April 1997 David Hucknall

Kennett is on the line between Bury St Edmunds and either Ely or Newmarket (the line divides just to the north-east of Newmarket). The signal-box, painted grey, is a Great Eastern Railway Type 2 of 1880. The roof, with a significant overhang, has plain bargeboards and no finials, typical of Type 2 'boxes. The absence of any glazing bars in the windows is unusual compared to that of contemporary signal-boxes from other companies.

On the evening this photograph was taken, Kennett signal-box was deserted, not intentionally, but because the signalman had been driven out by a swarm of bees. Help was on its way.

3 May 1995 David Hucknall

The signalman at Littleport returns to his 'box after reopening the gate to road traffic. Littleport is on the King's Lynn, Wisbech and Ely line. Between Littleport and Queen Adelaide, it runs close to the River Ouse across the flat fenland.

The signal-box was opened in 1882 by the Great Eastern Railway. It is a Type 2 timber 'box, its gable roof having a considerable overhang and plain bargeboards.

3 May 1995 David Hucknall

Shepreth Branch Junction signal-box used to lie 55¼ miles from King's Cross at a point where the line from Hitchin to Cambridge joins the Liverpool Street–Cambridge main line. Prior to the Grouping, Shepreth Branch Junction was owned by the Great Eastern Railway. The 'box appears to be an example of a post-1888 GE Type 7 (*The Signal-Box*, 1986) with its operating floor window three panes deep, plain bargeboards and a stovepipe chimney.

Lawrence James

Not the usual view of the signal-box at Brandon in Norfolk, this photograph shows the rear of the 'box from a viewpoint looking towards the Great Eastern Hotel with its beautifully painted sign. Brandon 'box is 16 miles from Ely and oversees the crossing of the former GER to Thetford and Norwich by the B1106/A1065. At Brandon crossing, the two roads come together and then separate. The extension to the 'box aids visibility considerably.

According to the *Signal-Box Directory* (1992), the signal-box may have been opened by the LNER in 1931. Said to be a Type 11C, some of the features certainly suggest a 1930s 'box. I was informed at the time of this photograph that each Sunday a former signalman at Brandon would remove and polish all the lever identification plates, including the screws.

May 1995 David Hucknall

Although no longer in use, the signal-box at Southend (Victoria) remains a feature of the station. Opened in 1889, it is a Type 8 'box, a design used by the Great Eastern Railway during 1888/9 on the 'New Essex Lines' (*The Signal-Box*, 1986).

Over the years, the 'box has changed gradually. A close examination of the photograph shows the subtle decoration on the fascia and bargeboards but the roof itself, which once had terracotta finials and decorative ridge tiles, has obviously been replaced. The locking-room windows were bricked up over forty years ago.

5 September 1996 David Hucknall

(*Opposite, top*) A line between Sheffield and Manchester via Penistone and Woodhead Tunnel was opened on 22 December 1845 by the Sheffield, Ashton-under-Lyne and Manchester Railway. The latter concern become part of the Manchester, Sheffield and Lincolnshire Railway in 1846 and, by 1849, trains were running between Manchester, Grimsby and New Holland. Branch lines from Penistone subsequently followed – Penistone to Huddersfield opened on 1 July 1850, while the MSLR line to Barnsley opened for goods as far as Dodworth in 1854.

After the MSLR became the Great Central Railway in 1897 and opened its London extension in 1899, Penistone became prominent in the GCR's attempts to capture traffic between the West Riding and London from the Midland and the Great Northern. To deal with increasing coal traffic, the GCR also opened the marshalling yard at Wath-on-Dearne in 1907. The Wath–Penistone freight-only line was subsequently used to shift heavy loads of South Yorkshire coal to the North West via Mottram yards.

Penistone once had three signal-boxes, North, Huddersfield Junction and Barnsley Junction. Shown here is Barnsley Junction 'box on a typical, edge-of-the-Pennines winter day. A large 90-lever 'box, it controlled the area where the Barnsley branch diverged from the Sheffield–Manchester line. Its levers operated signals (ground and semaphore) and points on both routes, including the associated goods lines and shunting sidings.

Obviously a former MSLR 'box, its height was necessary to give signal staff a good view over a complex layout of lines.

Lawrence James

Former Great Central Railway Lines

Sheffield–Manchester

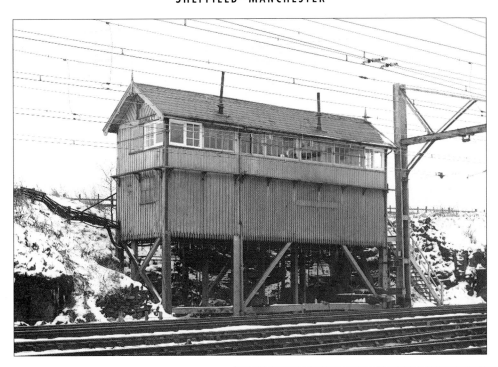

The signal-box at Penistone station was formerly Penistone's 'Huddersfield Junction' signal-box. It was opened in 1888 and is a modified version of the Manchester, Sheffield and Lincolnshire Railway Type 2 design.

It is seen here from the Sheffield end of what had been the 'branch' platforms, as opposed to the main Sheffield–Manchester platforms. The 'box seems isolated among the scrubby bushes which now grow where trains hauled by electric locomotives once hummed by.

4 October 1996 David Hucknall

Torside Crossing was 7.1 miles west of Dunford Bridge on the cross-Pennine route to Manchester via Penistone and Woodhead. It was only one of two crossings (the other was at Beighton) on the Great Central Railway between Manchester and Marylebone. Torside signal-box was at a point on the route where the gradient was 1 in 117/100.

Torside signal-box was in the style of Great Central 'boxes elsewhere. It was made of wood and had a finialled slate roof. The bargeboards had simple decoration. At the top of the stairs, a porch protected the entrance to the 'box. The exact date of this photograph isn't known but, by this time, the gallery which was fitted to the front of the 'box above the locking-room windows had been removed. One clue to the date is the fact that, behind the 'box, a 400kV pylon and cables can be seen. These were part of a system energized in 1969 and joined a supply that was laid through the original Up tunnel between Dunford and Woodhead.

Lawrence James

The grey-painted, timber-built former Great Central Railway Type 5 signal-box at Shireoaks East Junction. Opened in 1914, this 35-lever 'box plays an important role in the control of rail traffic to the west of Worksop station (D. Allen. *Changing Signals at Worksop*, Rail (295), 28 (1997)), overseeing the Up and Down yards and the double junction between Sheffield and Shirebrook lines. Over 100 Type 5 'boxes were built over a period of approximately 30 years (1900–1930). Although apparently trim and well-kept, the 'box is structurally weak and is beginning to list towards the Up sidings.

It is almost impossible to photograph the 'box without trespassing on Railtrack property. I am immensely grateful to Brian Bates, the Signalling Manager for Railtrack at Worksop, for his assistance in taking this and other photographs in the area.

13 January 1997 David Hucknall

Passing the signal-box at Edwinstowe station is 'K3' class 2–6–0 no. 61976 heading the 2.38 p.m. (Saturdays only) Shirebrook North-Ollerton train. Edwinstowe was originally on the Lancashire, Derbyshire and East Coast Railway.

The LD&ECR was planned as a coal-carrying railway which would allow transportation of coal from north-east Derbyshire either to the Manchester Ship Canal or to Sutton-on-Sea, where a port was planned. Engineering difficulties and a chronic shortage of money curtailed the 'West-to-East' route so that, by the end of 1896, it only ran between Chesterfield and Pyewipe Junction near Lincoln.

The LD&ECR had thirty signal-boxes dating from 1896–8. From Chesterfield to Tuxford, they were built by Saxby and Farmer. With decorated bargeboards, two gable-end windows and operating-floor windows three panes deep, Edwinstowe 'box was a typical S and F example. According to the Signalling Study Group (*The Signal-Box*, 1986, p. 128). Tuxford Central was the last LD&ECR 'box in use, closing in 1984.

28 August 1961 David Holmes

The left-hand and balanced bracket signals that stand side by side near Shireoaks East Junction signal-box dominate this photograph. They control movements on the Down main and Down departure no. 1 lines west of Worksop.

On the morning of Monday 13 January 1997, a train, having left Worksop, dashes past on the Down line. The 'off' home arm for the Down main is controlled by Shireoaks East Junction 'box. The distant arm is controlled by Shireoaks station.

13 January 1997 David Hucknall

The 'box at Shireoaks station is one of five in the Worksop area due to be closed over a two-year period, starting in May 1997. This is as a result of 'EROS' (Early Reduction of Signal-boxes), a proposal of Railtrack London and North Eastern Zone.

Photographed here from a platform of the derelict station, the much-modified Saxby and Farmer 'box was opened for the MSLR in 1874. It was fitted with individual function switches in 1980. As well as the barriers for the road crossing, it operates colour-light signals on several lines, including one from Shireoaks East towards Woodend Junction, and the single line from Woodend towards Shireoaks station.

2 October 1994 David Hucknall

Worksop East signal-box stands at the Retford end of Worksop station. It overlooks the crossing of the Retford–Sheffield line by the road that leads from the A60 to what is euphemistically signposted as the 'town centre'.

Identified as a Type 2 'box of the Manchester, Sheffield and Lincolnshire Railway (*The Signal-Box*, 1986), it was opened sometime during the period 1880-7. The present 20-lever McKenzie and Holland signalling frame was, however, fitted as recently as 1975 and was originally installed at Sleaford Junction 'box, Boston. Worksop East controls the line from the east end of the station to Manton Colliery Junction with colour lights operated by the lever frame. Worksop West signal-box at the Sheffield end of the station, supervises the Up and Down main lines as far as Shireoaks East Junction, together with the associated Down reception sidings.

5 September 1994 David Hucknall

The right-hand bracket signal which stands by the side of the Down main line near Worksop West signal-box is seen here. The stop and distant signals refer to the main line while the shorter of the miniature arm signals refers to the Down reception no. 2 siding. The taller of the miniatures refers to the Down reception no. 1 siding. The removal of semaphore signals such as these is inevitable with the planned resignalling of this area under Railtrack LNE Zone's EROS scheme. It is nevertheless regrettable to the enthusiast.

October 1994 David Hucknall

The signal-box at Clipstone West Junction dates from 1917. It was built by the Railway Signal Company for the Great Central Railway, according to a design categorized as Type 5. This was used until 1930 and over one hundred examples were made.

Built of timber (as almost three quarters of them were), Clipstone West Junction 'box has three large locking-room windows (three panes deep by three panes across). Although the central three windows are fixed, sliding sections are fitted next to the corner posts. These are sections of two panes which slide behind fixed sections.

13 January 1997 David Hucknall

Maltby Colliery South signal-box (an ex-GCR box of 1912). Maltby Main Colliery was one of five collieries (Dinnington Main, Firbeck Main, Markham Main and Harworth were the others) once served by the South Yorkshire Joint Railway. The SYJR arose from the desire by five railway companies (the GCR, GNR, NER, Midland Railway and the L&YR) to gain access to the rich coalfield centred on Maltby. The line ran from Dinnington Junction to Kirk Sandall Junction via Maltby, Tickhill and Black Carr. Maltby South was one of thirteen signal-boxes that existed on this line (others included St Catherine's Junction (50 levers), Potteric Carr, Firbeck 'A' and 'B', Maltby North and South etc.).

In the 1930s, the number of freight trains coming on and off the SYJR numbered about thirty-six per day in each direction.

1 October 1994 David Hucknall

Signals on the former South Yorkshire Joint Railway seen in thawing snow. The SYJR opened for mineral traffic in 1909. It runs from Dinnington Colliery Junction to Kirk Sandall Junction. From 1¾ miles north of Dinnington to near Tickhill, the line climbs at a gradient of 1 in 113. Of the signals that are visible, the left-hand bracket signal controls the main line and the shunting signal refers to the line leading to Maltby Colliery which can be seen in the background.

28 January 1995 David Hucknall

A standard LNER ground disc signal, consisting of a white metal disc with a red horizontal band. Also visible, just behind the disc, is the top of the oil lamp holder used to illuminate the signal aspect. Ground signals control shunting movements over crossovers or through connections between running lines and yards. This example is located just beyond Shireoaks East Junction signal-box to control main line–yard movements.

David Hucknall

Gainsborough Central was on the Great Grimsby and Sheffield Junction Railway that ran from Grimsby via Barnetby, Brigg and Kirton-in-Lindsey.

The signal-box remains in reasonably good condition. A Manchester, Sheffield and Lincolnshire Railway Type 2 'box of 1885, it retains some typical features. The gabled ends have diagonally arranged battens while the bargeboards have simple roundels and spikelets. The large gable-end window (here boarded up) was a standard feature of later MSLR/GCR designs. Beneath the windows, now protected with wire, the vertical boarding that extends to ground level on the Type 2 'box at Worksop East has been abruptly curtailed.

19 November 1994 David Hucknall

Elsham signal-box stands guard over the B1206 road between Elsham village and Brigg and the railway line between Wrawby Junction and Scunthorpe. Opened in 1885, the signal-box was built by the Railway Signal Co. for the MS&L Railway. Standing to the left of the crossing are the remains of Elsham station. It was opened on 1 October 1866 for the Trent, Ancholme and Grimsby Railway and closed by the British Railways Board on 4 October 1993.

2 July 1995 David Hucknall

Ulceby is on the original line between Grimsby and New Holland completed on 1 March 1848 by the Manchester, Sheffield and Lincolnshire Railway as part of the Great Grimsby and Sheffield Junction Railway scheme. The Ulceby–Brigg and Barnetby–Market Rasen sections followed on 1 November 1848. It stands now as the northern apex of a triangular arrangement of lines with Barnetby and Habrough at the other corners.

Ulceby Junction (or Ulceby South Junction, as given on the nameboard at the front) signal-box is a Great Central Railway Type 5. This variant was the GCR's final design for signal-boxes. It was opened in 1910 and has a GCR/McKenzie and Holland frame, reduced from its original size to 30 levers. In this view it was painted in a light grey with dark grey steps, handrails and guards. The bargeboards are deeper than in previous designs, with two roundels.

2 July 1995 David Hucknall

Brigg is on the line that runs between Gainsborough, Grimsby and Cleethorpes. It once had a station with an overall roof and its main buildings were 'grand affairs in the Italianate style' (P. Anderson. *The Railways of Lincolnshire*, Irwell Press, 1992). Nowadays, Brigg is poorly served by the railway, with just three trains on Saturdays only running to and from Grimsby and Cleethorpes.

Brigg's signal-box was opened in 1885. It was built for the Manchester, Sheffield and Lincolnshire Railway by the Railway Signalling Co. When seen in 1995, it was in very good condition. The bargeboards, finials and window frames were painted white while the rest of the woodwork was a pleasant grey-brown shade. One slight difference from this view is that the rear bargeboards were plain with a scalloped edge, not perforated with spikelets as seen here.

Lawrence James

Details of the upper end elevation of Beighton station signal-box. The date of the opening of the 'box is uncertain. The bargeboards with the roundels were used extensively and over a long period by the MS&L/GCR. The relatively small spikes as embellishments, however, suggest a date after 1887/8 (*The Signal-Box*, 1986). The brick base would also indicate a Type 4 but the absence of locking-room windows and a brick chimney are less typical.

2 October 1994 David Hucknall

The signal-box at Kiveton Park station stands on the other side of the level crossing from the eastern end of the station. A Great Central Type 5 structure, its date of opening does not seem to be known (Kay, 1997). It works under absolute block regulations with Woodhouse Junction to the west and Brancliffe Junction – where the former South Yorkshire Joint line joins the main line – to the east.

Under the EROS scheme, which will remove most of the signal-boxes around Worksop, the new Worksop signal-box will have Kiveton Park station as a fringe 'box on the main line to Sheffield.

15 December 1996 David Hucknall

LONDON MIDLAND REGION

Immediately after the formation of the London, Midland and Scottish Railway in 1923, civil engineering, which included signalling in that company, was dealt with on a divisional basis. In England, the centres were at Derby, Crewe and Manchester. Derby tended to deal with the former Midland Railway lines, Crewe with those of the LNWR and the Furness and North Staffordshire Railway, while Manchester handled L&YR matters. Under this system, the practices of the constituent companies of the LMSR continued without much modification. Consolidation started in 1929 with the appointment of A.F. Bound as the first Chief Signal and Telegraph Engineer. One of Bound's first directives was that lower quadrant signals, typical of the consituents, should be gradually replaced by upper quadrant ones (some superb examples of lower quadrant signals, however, survived well into the 1960s).

Although mechanical signalling has been massively curtailed on the former London Midland Region and even upper quadrant semaphores are to be found only on a few lines, the number of pre-Grouping and 'traditional' signal-boxes that still exist is surprisingly high. The 'classic' standard Midland Railway 'box, invariably made throughout of wood and with hipped roofs and finials of a design that was used both on 'boxes and signals, can still be found. Many are in very good condition. The Hellifield–Carlisle, Newark–Nottingham and Syston–Peterborough lines have some excellent examples.

The LNWR had its own signal works at Crewe from 1875 where it made its own characteristic equipment. In contrast with the Midland's neat little signal-boxes, the LNWR's structures could hardly be classified as handsome. They had brick bases and wooden upper works.. Certainly with Type 4s, that were made for almost thirty years, ornamentation was kept to a minimum. The gable ends were plain and unadorned, the bargeboards were set directly over the boarding and had fairly simple finials. Inside, with 'boxes that retain LNWR equipment, the most noticeable feature is the large levers with their ugly stirrup-like catches mounted at the front. The LNWR liked big 'boxes and even now, structures such as Stockport no. 2 (page 54) still impress.

Relatively few Lancashire and Yorkshire signal-boxes now remain. By the end of 1995, there were some thirty-five examples of which seven served the former L&YR routes around Manchester. The survivors reflect past L&YR practice. Between 1881 and 1891, the railway used contractors to perform its signalling work. It was only in 1890 that it began to manufacture its own equipment at Horwich. Of the exisiting ex-L&YR 'boxes illustrated in this chapter, Hensall was built by Yardley, Brierfield by Saxby and Farmer, while Hebden Bridge, Crigglestone Junction and the remainder were L&YR built. With the exception of the Great Western Railway, most railway companies identified their signal-boxes merely with a statement of its location. The L&YR, however, sometimes added the word 'cabin' after the location. Parbold Cabin is an example of this.

Of the pre-Grouping railway companies that initially formed the LMSR and, on nationalization, the London Midland region of British Railways, only the Cheshire Lines Railway and the North Staffordshire Railway have been included in this book. The latter organization built 'boxes with steeply pitched roofs and overhanging eaves. Mow Cop signal-box is a very good example. The CLR which, at the outbreak of the Second World War owned or worked approximately 144 route miles of railway, initially relied on contractors for its signalling work. In 1885, it began to manufacture locking frames and other equipment at its works in Warrington. The examples shown here are CLR built and showing their age. It is staggering to realise, however, that Northenden Junction retains its original nameboard after almost a century.

'Conventional' 'boxes were built by the LMR up to the late 1940s. These were usually LMSR standard designs, recommended by the Railway Executive Committee. The appearance of REC 'boxes such as Stanlow and Nantwich, for example, are typical. Later LMR practice produced reasonable-looking 'boxes, e.g. Hest Bank, but recent trends have no such architectural merit whatsoever. The thought of a railway system with structures such as Rufford or Sandhills Merseyrail signal-box is depressing indeed.

Stockport no. 2 signal-box is a LNWR Type 4 opened in 1890. It has a 90-lever frame but this is a reduced version of the original. It works by the AB system with Heaton Norris Junction to the north and Stockport no. 1 'box at the south end of the station. The Stockport 'boxes, together with Edgeley Junction no. 1 and Cheadle Hulme, have a combined age of 540 years.

David Hucknall

FORMER LNWR LINES

EUSTON–CREWE

Signal WJ 222, controlled by the power signal-box at Watford Junction, stands by the side of the Down main line at Berkhamsted station. In the foreground, the milepost indicates that the station is 28 miles from Euston. Watford Junction PSB controls 28 route miles of the West Coast main line and when it opened in 1964, ten mechanical signal-boxes (including Berkhamsted) were replaced.

David Hucknall

Lichfield Trent Valley no. 1 signal-box dominates the north end of the station. It is an LNWR Type 5 'box, opened in 1911. Its bargeboards and finials are painted an attractive shade of light blue, while the remaining woodwork is white. In LNWR days, cabins were painted buff and medium brown. The bargeboards, finials, window frames and ironwork were brown, the window frames white and the remaining woodwork buff (R.D. Foster. *A Pictorial History of LNWR Signalling*, 1982).

The nameboard of the 'box is in maroon enamel with white lettering and perpetuates the LNWR tradition of numbering 'boxes with the lowest number at the London end of the station.

1 April 1997 David Hucknall

Hademore Crossing signal-box lies 113 miles and 40 chains from Euston on the Tamworth–Rugby section of the Trent Valley line. An example of a LNWR Type 4a 'box, it was opened in 1899. It has a 15-lever frame.

1 April 1997 David Hucknall

The layout of the railway lines near Edgeley Junction no. 2 signal-box can be seen in this photograph taken from a train passing on the Down fast line. To the left of the signal-box is the Down slow line. Coming in from the right are the lines to Northenden Junction and the Glazebrook to Godley line.

In the right background, some 390 yards away, is Edgeley Junction no. 1 'box (no. 1 because, in LNWR tradition, it is nearer Euston) which oversees the line to Hazel Grove and the Buxton Branch.

Both of the Edgeley Junction signal-boxes are Type 4s of the LNWR, dating from 1884. Consisting of timber tops on brick bases, Type 4 'boxes such as these were built from about 1876 to 1904. According to Foster (*A Pictorial Record of LNWR Signalling*, 1982), '. . . many hundreds of cabins of this design were erected and, after about 1890, it was by far the most common design found on the LNWR and its successors'.

David Hucknall

Details of the London end of Stockport no. 1 signal-box. It stands at the end of platform 4 of the station. Opened in 1884, it was originally one of the ubiquitous LNWR Type 4 cabins and classified as size 'P': 54 ft 1½ ins long and a 90-lever frame. (*A Pictorial Record of LNWR Signalling*, 1982) Extended in 1910, by 15 ft 6 ins at one end and 7 ft 9 ins at the other, its frame size was also increased.

Stockport no. 1, together with the two Edgeley Junction 'boxes and Stockport no. 2, survived the Manchester Piccadilly–Crewe resignalling mentioned in the Introduction. A recent article by David Allen (*Rail*, no. 297, January/February 1997, p. 34) observed, 'Stockport is destined to be the only location where Eurostars will be "belled on" in the time-honoured tradition'.

David Hucknall

The signal-box at Mow Cop is not easy to find. It lies quite near Little Moreton Hall on a small road leading to a minor road which joins the A34. It is 11.3 miles from Macclesfield station and guards a level-crossing on the former North Staffordshire Railway's line between there and Stoke-on-Trent.

The NSR had once been a 'go-ahead, prosperous concern' (R. Keys. 'The Plunder of the North Staffordshire', *Trains Illustrated*, 9 (10), 504 (1956)). At the Grouping, it was acquired by the LMS which acted, over subsequent years, according to Keys, as ' . . . the official receivers'. It had opened a station at Mow Cop in October 1848 which was closed by British Railways in September 1964. The opening date of the signal-box is not known (*The Signal-Box Directory*, 1992). The design is that of a NSR Type 2 'box, with operating floor windows three panes deep and sliding sashes by the front corner posts only but this design was used from the mid-1880s to the Grouping.

April 1996 David Hucknall

Meaford Crossing signal-box (*c.* 1880) is situated fairly close to Stone station. It stands in the V formed by the divergence at Stone of the former North Staffordshire Railway's principal routes between Stoke-on-Trent, Norton Bridge and Stafford and Stoke and Colwich. Stone station was built in the Jacobean style according to a design by H.A. Hunt. In this three-quarter view of Meaford Crossing 'box its exceedingly tall chimney and ornamental bargeboards can be clearly seen. The nameboard is in dark maroon enamel with white lettering.

According to the Hendrys (R. Preston Hendry and R. Powell Hendry. *An Historical Survey of Selected LMS Stations*, vol. I, Poole, OPC, 1982), in 1978 the 'box had a 26-lever frame of which 14 were working. By 1992, it had been reduced in size to a 16-lever frame.

April 1996 David Hucknall

Abergele and Pensarn station is on the former Chester and Holyhead Railway that sweeps close to the North Wales Coast between Llandudno and Rhyl.

The signal-box at Abergele was opened in 1902 when the station was enlarged as a result of the conversion of the railway line from two to four tracks. It was situated at the Chester end of the platforms between the Up and Down fast lines to give the best possible view of railway activities. A former LNWR Type 4 'box (a design that emerged from the Signalling Department at Crewe Works from 1876 to 1904), it has a 60-lever frame with bar and stud locking.

The Up fast line was removed in December 1988 and the sidings which were on both sides of the station are long gone.

April 1996 Sarah Turvey

Now disused and a Grade II listed building, the former Rhyl no. 2 signal-box stands some 18 feet above rail level at the western end of the station. The height was very necessary to give the signalman a good view over what, some forty years ago, was a complex and busy railway layout (Rhyl locomotive shed was located just beyond the 'box, approximately where the building labelled 'Crosville' stands). The 'box was opened in 1900 and is a LNWR Type 4. In the days when Rhyl station had a platform awning, it had a cantilevered cabin built out at the west end to help visibility.

April 1996 Sarah Turvey

A distant view of Prestatyn signal-box looking south-west. The branch to Dyserth, closed in September 1993, used to enter from the left, behind the 'box. The remains of the bracket home signals used to control the platform line, adjacent to platform 1 at Prestatyn station and the branch siding, can also be seen.

April 1996 Sarah Turvey

Prestatyn signal-box was opened in 1897. A LNWR Type 4, it has a 45-lever frame and LNWR tumbler locking. Apart from traffic on its section of the Chester–Holyhead line, Prestatyn 'box was also responsible for traffic on the Dyserth branch. Now it functions only to break up a block section.

April 1996 Sarah Turvey

The signal-box at Beeston Castle and Tarporley is on the former Crewe and Chester Railway line, 10 miles 51 chains from Chester. It was built by the LNWR in 1915.

Against a background of the attractive countryside of the Cheshire Plain this Type 5 box looks solid and reassuring. When compared to the earlier Type 4s, the LNWR Type 5 boxes (*The Signal-Box*, 1986) have features which make them visually very attractive. The overhanging roof, the windows 6-feet deep, even the stair-top outside toilet with its finialled roof; all contribute to its appeal.

Since its commissioning in 1984, Chester power signal-box has worked TCB (Track Circuit Block) on the line as far as Beeston Castle.

20 June 1994 David Hucknall

One of two ex-LNWR signal gantries and the end elevation of no. 4 signal-box can be seen here. This shows a Stanier 'Black Five' no. 45437 approaching Chester General station with an Up mixed freight.

Chester no. 4 signal-box was large. Opened in 1904, it had an LNWR 176-lever frame built by that railway according to the design of F.W. Webb. Webb frames had levers with front-mounted stirrups instead of the rear-mounted catch handles seen elsewhere in this book. Chester no. 4 used to control the convergence of the Holyhead lines with the Birkenhead route. The superb LNWR signals were abolished in early 1981 when the track area between no. 4 and no. 3A 'boxes was reorganized and resignalled.

31 May 1966 David Holmes

It is a surprise to realise that the wooden signal-box at Nantwich station was built by British Railways as late as 1954. It is of a standard pattern introduced by H.E. Morgan. He had been with the Signalling Department of the Midland Railway at Derby but was moved to Crewe in 1927 (*A Pictorial Record of LMS Signals*, Oxford, Oxford Publishing Co., 1972). Morgan set about designing a standard signal-box for the LMS almost immediately and the first examples began to appear in 1928. Nantwich was one of the last examples and incorporates a second-hand lever frame from Wem North.

Nantwich has changed over the years. It retains its cockscomb ridge tiles, but the window cleaning stage at the front was removed in August 1985 when alterations were made, including the installation of lifting barriers to protect the Nantwich–Whitchurch Road.

23 April 1996 David Hucknall

An interior view of Nantwich station signal-box.

David Hucknall

An isolated signal-box, Wrenbury 'box is 8 miles and 52 chains from Crewe South Junction on the Crewe–Shrewsbury line. It is a LNWR Type 4 structure dating from 1882. This design of signal-box is not particularly eye-catching, having plain bargeboards fitting closely to the cabin boarding. They also had fixed glazing and walkways were provided for cleaning the outside of the windows. This is clearly shown here.

24 April 1996 David Hucknall

(*Opposite, top*) A brief burst of winter sunlight illuminates Prees signal-box and standing by the door is the duty signalman, Barry Cank.

Prees is a LNWR Type 4 cabin opened in 1881. It stands on the former LNWR line between Shrewsbury and Crewe in flat, fertile Shropshire countryside and guards a very minor road that links the B5476 with the A49. Prees station, 18 miles and 39 chains from Crewe South Junction, closed to goods traffic in October 1969 although the loading gauge remains.

22 January 1997 David Hucknall

A view inside Prees signal-box showing part of the 25-lever LNWR frame. The Webb frame, with its stirrup catch handles at the front, was unique to the LNWR. A comment has been made (R. Preston Hendry and R. Powell Hendry. *The Steam Age in Colour*, Blandford Press, Poole, 1985) that 'North Western men swore by them; most other men simply swore at them'. The console from which the crossing barriers are operated can also be seen by the window.

David Hucknall

Hest Bank is the only place where the West Coast main line actually gets close to the sea. It then turns inland again, heading for either Lancaster or Carnforth. It once had a station, which closed to passengers on 3 February 1969 and a small goods yard which closed on 2 December 1963. The latter was subsequently used for green and white camping coaches that looked out across the hazardous waters of Morecambe Bay.

The present signal-box, Hest Bank level-crossing frame as it is named, opened in 1958 and stands on the seaward side of railway lines, guarding the crossing of a spur from the A5105. It is a pleasant-looking 'box, built on a red-brown brick base, with an overhanging roof. It replaced the former LNWR signal-box that had stood 165 yards further south at the end of the Up platform of the station.

28 October 1996 David Hucknall

(*Opposite, top*) At the west end of Narborough station, the line crosses a public road on the other side of which were coal and goods yards. In this photograph, the signal-box (a LNWR Type 3 of 1875) oversees the crossing while, in the background, the former goods shed still stands. Narborough's pleasant cast-iron footbridge is also intact.

Narborough station has led a precarious existence. In March 1968, all the stations between Nuneaton and Leicester were closed, with the exception of Hinckley. Only through the intervention of the Friends of Narborough Station, did it escape demolition in 1969. On 4 January 1970, after a long battle, and on payment of several thousand pounds, Blaby Rural Council persuaded British Railways to reopen Narborough for a three-year experimental period.

15 December 1995 David Hucknall

The former LNWR signal cabin at Hazel Grove is on the Up platform of the station, 2 miles and 21 chains from Edgeley Junction no. 1 'box. Classified as a Type 4 cabin, it was opened in 1877. When this photograph was taken, it had cream/white woodwork with dark–red corner posts, bargeboards and finials.

Looking along the platform, beyond the colour-light signal HG 18, the divergence of the Hazel Grove chord from the Up Buxton line can be seen. The former leads to New Mills and the Hope Valley line.

1 November 1994 David Hucknall

After a day of heavy rain, the setting sun illuminates the end of Stanlow and Thornton signal cabin. It was once a busy 'box controlling movements on the line between Frodsham and Hooton and the South sidings and filling racks of Shell's Stanlow refinery. Now it sees relatively little use.

Classified as an LMS Type 11c 'box, it was opened in 1941. It has the cockscomb ridge tiles which are uncommon.

26 February 1997 David Hucknall

The signal-box at Bare Lane stands at the end of the Down Heysham goods line. It dates from 1937 and is an LMS Type 11c and stands 57 chains from Morecambe South Junction on the West Coast main line. In this photograph, Bare Lane level-crossing can be seen just beyond the platform end.

Just beyond the eastern end of the station, at Bare Lane Junction, the line divides into two single line curves. The shorter south curve leads to Morecambe South Junction while the other leads to Hest Bank Junction.

28 October 1996 David Hucknall

FORMER L&YR LINES

PRESTON–BLACKPOOL

Rain glistens on the platforms at Blackpool Central station. Even as late as 1963, Blackpool was served by thirty terminal platforms that came into their own for a short time each year with excursions from a wide area of the north of England and the Midlands to see the 'Illuminations'.

On this wet April morning, very little is moving and all the signals are 'on'. Dominating the right-hand background of the photograph, however, is the 138-lever signal-box that oversaw operations within the station.

17 April 1963 DavidHucknall

WIGAN–ORMSKIRK

The level-crossing at Parbold, seen from the entrance to the station platforms. Parbold Cabin, as the overseeing signal-box is named, is on the former L&YR Wigan and Southport line, 24 miles and 49 chains from Manchester Victoria.

The nameboard of the 'box may be original. It is painted dark red with the lettering picked out in white.

13 December 1996 David Hucknall

Hensall station is 16½ miles from Wakefield on the former Wakefield, Pontefract and Goole Railway. From Knottingley, the line was built across flat, uninteresting land, following approximately the course of the Knottingley and Goole Canal to Whitley Bridge. From there the line headed due east, through Hensall station, before turning east-south-east towards Hensall Junction to avoid the meandering River Aire.

Hensall station is well cared for. At the west end of the station, there is a level-crossing for the road between Hensall village and the A645 to the south. The ex L&YR signal-box stands slightly behind the end of the platform for Leeds-bound trains. A rather plain 'box, it was built by E.S. Yardley and Sons of Manchester and opened in 1875. As can be seen from this photograph, the 'box retains many original features – the upper lights, four-pane windows and the two locking-room windows. Unfortunately, the colour-light signal significantly obscures much of the north elevation.

9 July 1996 David Hucknall

Barnsley station junction signal-box was opened in 1901. It was showing its ninety-four years of age when photographed from one of the platforms of Barnsley Interchange railway station.

Barnsley used to be an example of a medium-sized town rather over-provided with railway facilities as a result of pre-grouping rivalry. The Great Central Railway and the L&YR came into Exchange station while the Midland entered at Court House station from Sheffield via the Chapeltown branch.

When the Sheffield district of the Eastern region was reorganized in April 1960, Court House station was closed and provision made for a new connection (Quarry Junction) from the Chapeltown branch to Barnsley Exchange.

4 June 1995 David Hucknall

The signal-box at Crigglestone Junction. It is now boarded up and used only when required. The 'box is one of relatively few now surviving from the days of the Lancashire and Yorkshire Railway (the pre-grouping situation is summarized in booklets by T.T. Sutcliffe, for example, *L and YR Traffic Control Maps*, vol. 4, Yorkshire 1922, published in 1984).

Opened in 1901, Crigglestone Junction 'box is an example of an L&YR manufactured 'box. Prior to 1890, the L&YR used signalling contractors. It has 32 levers and stands at the southerly apex of a triangular arrangement of lines. To the north-west lies Horbury station junction leading to Healey Mills Yard. Horbury Junction is to the north-east.

18 March 1995 David Hucknall

The signal-box at Brierfield, near Nelson, was built by Saxby and Farmer for the Lancashire and Yorkshire Railway and opened in 1876. At that time, the L&YR bought in all its signalling equipment and, in 1876, Saxby and Farmer built twenty-five 'boxes for the L&YR compared to two supplied by E.S. Yardley & Co. and one from Stevens and Sons. Identified as Saxby and Farmer Type 8 (*The Signal-Box Directory*, 1992), it has arched locking-room windows and main windows consisting of two by two glass panes, small eaves brackets and a hipped roof. Although fitted in 1986 with an individual function switch panel, the disused L&YR frame of 1902 is said to be still retained in the 'box.

2 June 1996 David Hucknall

Huncoat Station Level Crossing Frame photographed from the station footbridge. Opened by the Lancashire and Yorkshire Railway in 1902, it lies immediately to the west of Huncoat station.

The original station lay on the line from Accrington to Burnley that went on to either Todmorden or Colne and then Skipton. The line was originally constructed as the Blackburn, Burnley, Accrington and Colne Extension Railway by the East Lancashire Railway and was acquired by the L&YR in 1859. The present Huncoat station stands some 745 m due south of the original.

24 April 1996 David Hucknall

The former Lancashire and Yorkshire Railway signal-box at Ashton Moss North Junction is a fine-looking structure which was opened in 1911. It has a 56-lever frame and appears to be made up to standard timber and glass sections, eight window panes wide and each with one two by two pane locking-room window.

Standing on the flat land on the west side of Ashton–under-Lyne, it overlooks a running track and playing fields. It is the sole survivor of three 'boxes (the other two being Ashton OA and GB Junction and Ashton Moss South Junction signal-boxes), that controlled a triangular arrangement of lines linking the former Oldham, Ashton-under-Lyne and Guide Bridge (OA and GBR) to the L&YR's Miles Platting–Stalybridge branch.

October 1996 David Hucknall

A close up of an end elevation of Ashton Moss North Junction signal-box.

October 1996 David Hucknall

A photograph of the splitting stop signals on the approach to Ashton Moss North Junction. The arm on the lower post controls traffic travelling from the Miles Platting–Stalybridge line to the Ashton and Guide Bridge line.

October 1996 David Hucknall

Hebden Bridge is on the former Lancashire and Yorkshire Railway line between Wakefield and Manchester. This climbs on almost unbroken gradients for 28½ miles from Horbury Junction to the east end of Summit Tunnel near Walsden.

The station and signal-box at Hebden Bridge are in a striking location, set between a steeply rising, wooded hillside to the south and the Rochdale Canal to the north. The station is obviously very well cared for and the signal-box is bright against the wooded hillside. Built in 1891, it is a former L&YR 'box and is identified with a cast-iron name-plate which, according to Warburton (*A Pictorial Record of LMS Signals*, 1972), is of L&YR origin. The 38-lever frame controls colour-light and semaphore signals and points. I was quite surprised to discover that it is also a fringe signal-box to the power 'box at Preston.

October 1996 David Hucknall

'Supersprinter' no. 156484 passes the signal-box at Stalybridge. The 'box is a Stevens/MSLR opened in 1886 (*The Signal-Box Directory*, 1992). It has quite a shallow pitched roof and also an unusual frame. Fitted in 1942, it is a Glasgow South Western Railway/LMS type and was made at Irvine in Ayrshire.

Stalybridge 'box is 7 miles 52 chains from Manchester Victoria, close to the point where the Huddersfield and Manchester line leads to either Ashton-under-Lyne and Miles Platting Junction or to Guide Bridge.

4 October 1996 David Hucknall

FORMER MIDLAND RAILWAY LINES

LEICESTER–MANTON JUNCTION

Melton Mowbray station is tucked away to the side of the A606 Oakham–Melton–Nottingham road. It is a small, rather cramped, two-platform station. Opened in 1942, Melton station 'box is unusual because of its height and overhang. This enabled the signalman to observe train movements in the sidings directly in front of and to the rear of the 'box. It is now painted light green and cream.

24 August 1996 David Hucknall

From Whissendine, the Up Syston and Peterborough line begins to climb gently at 1 in 261 for 3 miles. After crossing the former county boundary between Leicestershire and Rutland, the next signal-box on the line is Ashwell (96 miles and 67 chains from St Pancras via Corby).

Ashwell 'box is a former Midland Railway Type 4a. It was opened on 30 June 1912 as a replacement for an earlier structure dating from the mid-1870s. Several years ago, a short mineral branch ran from the station to the Cottesmore ironstone mines.

24 August 1996 David Hucknall

The signal-box at Langham Junction was opened on 27 October 1890 as Langham Crossing. It replaced a relatively short-lived 'box, 'Langham', that opened in 1881 and closed in March 1891. It is a former Midland Railway Type 2a and remains a handsome cabin.

From Langham Junction to Oakham, the line is level and there is a four-track section, the outermost lines being Up and Down goods loops. Langham Junction 'box and Oakham controlled the entrance and exit of the four-track section. In 1973, however, the Up goods loop was made a through siding and the Down goods line was worked 'no block'.

24 August 1996 David Hucknall

A view from the window of Langham Junction 'box looking towards Oakham. A train is passing by on the Up main line. Just beyond the leading vehicle, the entrance to the former Up goods loop can be seen and to the right the exit from the Down goods loop is visible.

June 1994 David Hucknall

The former Midland Railway's Syston and Peterborough line runs through the Vale of Catmose between Whissendine and Oakham. The signal-box at Whissendine is an interesting structure. It is a second-hand 'box, opened on the site in 1940 and can be identified as conforming to the Midland Railway's Type 4d patterns. This design was used up to 1928 by the Midland division of the LMSR. It was also at this time that brick bases began to be used.

The 20-lever frame at Whissendine, now virtually redundant, is a Railway Executive Committee version of the Midland Railway frame.

August 1996 David Hucknall

(*Opposite, top*) The signal-box at Oakham oversees the crossing of the railway by the A606 road. It is a former Midland Railway Type 2b, opened on 8 October 1899 as a replacement for an earlier structure dating from 1875. It has a 17-lever frame with MR tumbler locking. Oakham level-crossing signal-box is a listed building and may yet survive while others on the Melton line (Langham Junction, Ashwell, Whissendine) will probably be closed in the near future.

The Midland probably had the most distinctive design of signal-boxes of all the pre-Grouping companies. The 'box at Oakham was used as the basis for an Airfix model signal-box that was on sale during the 1960s.

25 July 1991 David Hucknall

(*Opposite, bottom*) A view from the site of Manton railway station shows the southern end of Manton Tunnel (length 749 yards) and Manton Junction signal-box. The track to the right is the former Midland Railway branch to Peterborough, realigned in July 1988. To the left is the remnant of the former double main line that passed through Harringworth, Geddington and Corby to Glendon South Junction and Kettering. This line, which had formed part of the through route between Nottingham and Kettering, was once used by through expresses, such as 'The Waverley' and its overnight equivalents, between London and Edinburgh.

The signal-box is essentially a Midland Railway Type 4c, opened on 9 November 1913. It replaced a 'box (opened 4 April 1886) which had superseded an even earlier structure (1 December 1879). According to Allen and Woolstenholmes (*A Pictorial Survey of London Midland Signalling*, (Oxford Publishing Co., 1996), p. 21) the 35-lever frame in the 'box was replaced during 1988 by an 'N-X' panel controlling colour-light signals.

August 1996 David Hucknall

The present station at Skipton was opened on 30 April 1876 by the Midland Railway. It replaced an earlier one in use since September 1847 and opened by the Leeds and Bradford Railway. It is a pleasant station with canopies, supported by ornate fanned ironwork and green and white painted columns, protecting the platforms. It was once a busy station which saw freight and passenger trains on their way to Carlisle and Leeds and beyond and useful local trains to Colne and Ilkley. It is now much quieter.

Perched precariously on his ladder, an engineer installs new signalling equipment. In the background is Skipton Station South signal-box, a Midland Type 3a, opened in 1906, and the semaphore signal controlling southbound departures from the station.

This was the last I saw of the 'box. I returned four months later to repeat the photograph only to be told it had been removed the previous December.

22 October 1994 David Hucknall

A view of Skipton Station North signal-box.
Howard Lorriman

Gargrave station, between Bell Busk and Skipton, was on the former Midland Railway line to Hellifield, Settle Junction and beyond. It was built by the 'Little' North Western Railway and its buildings were in its idiosyncratic style – in this case, a half-timbered 'cottage'. They were removed by British Rail in the 1960s. Here, 'Jubilee' class 4–6–0 no. 45598 *Basutoland*, passes the Up platform with a parcels train. At the end of the Down platform, the ex-MR signal-box can be seen. In the distance, in front of the overbridge, the Up home signal can just be made out. It was built exceedingly tall to be visible over the bridge.

27 September 1963 David Holmes

A view of the signal-box at Long Preston looking towards Settle Junction, from the bridge where Station Road crosses the railway. It shows the Midland Railway signal-box, with 4F no. 44197 passing with a Down class 9 freight. Of Long Preston, Dick Fawcett, who was appointed as a Class 1 relief signalman there in the early 1950s, said: 'It was a nice place to work. . . . An added attraction was that there were two lovely lady porters, both charming, pleasant girls.'

Long Preston was on the 'Little' North Western and opened in 1849. The Midland Railway took over the 'Little' in 1871 but it retained a character all of its own. To quote Donald Binns (1994), 'All the NWR stations were different but Long Preston was the oddest of the lot! It . . . was of wood construction, looking for all the world as if it had been built piecemeal by the local joiner.' The NWR buildings were demolished in the 1970s.

13 May 1964 David Holmes

According to an article on Midland signal-boxes (*Trains Illustrated*, 11 (117), p. 305, June 1958), 'If the box was visited by night, the most noticeable thing inside was the darkness . . . to help number recording, the box was kept as dark as possible, with just a feeble oil lamp shaded to shine on the train register book'. This oil lamp was still in use at Hellifield South signal-box in 1976.

January 1976 Nigel Mussett

The inside of Hellifield South Junction signal-box. It shows part of the 58-lever signal frame which dates from 1911. At the time of this photograph, the 'box controlled the main line between Settle Junction and Skipton station and the 'branch' line as far as Gisburn on the Blackburn route – the branch. Above the levers is the track diagram showing the location of the 'box at the end of the platform with the Up and Down main lines passing on either side.

January 1976 Nigel Mussett

At Settle Junction, the railway line divides. The Settle–Carlisle line begins to climb at 1 in 100. The other line, eventually leading to Morecambe, continues on the level but from the shadowing A65, it appears to fall away dramatically.

Guarding the junction is the former Midland Railway signal-box, Settle Junction, a MR Type 4c, opened in 1913. I was reminded of the fierce loyalties of railway staff when I saw an interview with Derek Soames, former signalman at Settle Junction on the BBC series, 'The Train Now Departing' made in 1987/8. He said 'we like to think if anybody said which line do you work on it's still the Midland. After all these years we still think of it as the Midland, even though the Midland finished in '22, and we've taken a pride in keeping this box as the Midland had it'. Derek Soames achieved his stated ambition of getting '50 years in on one firm'.

David Hucknall

Levers in typical ex-Midland Railway signal-boxes had their lower ends enclosed in a cover about 2 feet high, running the length of the frame. Lever pivots were set about floor level and the extent of lever movement was greater than that for levers with the pivot below the floor.

Midland Railway locking was fixed above floor level inside the casing, on the side away from the signalman and the top of this part of the casing carried a series of engraved plates with the lever description. In this photograph of levers inside the signal-box at Settle Junction such detail can be clearly seen. Attached to the front of each lever can be seen the identification plates giving the lever number, together with the numbers of the levers that have to be pulled first to free it. Signal repeaters (for signals 17 and 19) can be seen fixed to the front of the block shelf, almost over the lever concerned.

David Hucknall

Over the years, Settle has had more than its fair share of accidents. Some, such as that which befell the 9.5 p.m. Glasgow St Enoch to St Pancras in the early morning of 22 January 1959, have been unusual and very serious. In that case, the slide bar bolt on 'Britannia' class 4–6–2 worked loose and, 3 miles from Settle, the connecting and piston rods and crosshead dropped to the track, displacing sleepers and rails and derailing a northbound freight train.

This photograph, taken in May 1979, shows the derailed china clay train near Settle Junction signal-box. Smashed and overturned wagons and piles of china clay litter the track. The signal-box and the junction bracket signal can be seen in the background together with the Healey Mills breakdown crane. At the time of the accident, it was rumoured that the train was going rather fast past the junction. That appears not to have been the case, nor was a hot axle-box suspected.

Nigel Mussett

Healey Mills breakdown crane removing crash debris near Settle Junction signal-box. Recovered wagons have been placed on the top of the embankment.

Nigel Mussett

The former 'Little North Western' line was intended to run from Skipton to Clapham and then up the Lune Valley to join the Lancaster and Carlisle Railway near Low Gill. A branch was planned from Clapham to Lancaster. In the end, the easier route to Lancaster became the 'main line'.

From Clapham, the line follows the River Wenning to Wennington. There, the line used to branch. The former Furness and Midland Railways' joint line went to Carnforth and served Melling, Arkholme-with-Cawood and Borwick. The other line ran to Hornby, Caton, Holton and Lancaster.

Wennington is now a mere shadow of what it must have been. The signal-box, Wennington Junction, stands deserted at the end of the Up platform. Opened by the Midland Railway in 1890, it is classified as a Type 2a.

28 October 1996 David Hucknall

When I visited Newark Castle station, on the ex-Midland Railway line between Nottingham and Lincoln, it was a disgrace. The approach, over sagging stone sets, was derelict and the buildings were boarded up. There was no way of getting between platforms except via the level-crossing at the Nottingham end of the station.

In contrast, the signal-box, guarding the crossing, is in a wonderful state of preservation. A Midland Railway Type 4a, opened in 1912, it is shown here with Type 56 diesel no. 56046 passing with a trainload of oil tanks.

8 July 1995 David Hucknall

Signalman Pinkett pauses at the window of Fiskerton Junction 'box. The 'box is built to a Midland Railway Type 4e design and was opened in 1929. Plainly visible are the typical MR 'box features – the gallery that runs round the front and sides of the 'box, provided for window cleaning, the short, vertical boarding to the base of the windows and the large windows themselves, chamfered in the top corners. The road crossing gates and that for pedestrians, together with the diagonal fencing, are probably just as they were forty or fifty years before.

8 July 1995 David Hucknall

The small signal-box at Fiskerton is 12 miles and 43 chains from Nottingham on the Nottingham–Lincoln line. Several other boxes, including Lowdham, Fiskerton Junction, Staythorpe Crossing and Newark Castle station, remain on this line. Fiskerton 'box controls the crossing of an unclassified road between Fiskerton village and Southwell. It was opened on 6 July 1902 as a replacement for an earlier (*c.* 1877) box.

The 'box retains the original 1902 16-lever frame. Inevitably, over the years, changes have been made to its appearance. The original three panels of three by three pane windows have been replaced with larger areas of glass. Further, the 'box once had two nameboards but the one which was below the front windows has been removed.

8 July 1995 David Hucknall

Staythorpe Crossing signal-box stands on a level-crossing on the Nottingham–Lincoln line. The road which crosses the railway runs approximately north-east to south-west up the valley of the River Trent towards Rolleston and Southwell.

The 'box and its surroundings seem quite rural but not far away are sidings that serve Staythorpe 'B' power station. Opened in 1950, but extended later, it is classified as a LMS Type 11c. It perpetuates in many ways characteristics of earlier 'boxes built by the Midland Railway.

8 July 1995 David Hucknall

Lincoln Street level-crossing, and Nottingham is 127 miles and 60 chains from St Pancras via Corby. Here, the B6004, Arnold–Stapleford road crosses the Mansfield line as it follows the valley of the River Leen.

The signal-box stands on the north side of the crossing. It is a 16-lever, Type 4a (1906–17) 'box opened by the Midland Railway in 1916 (probably as a replacement for an earlier structure). When opened, Lincoln Street Crossing 'box would have worked with Basford Siding signal-box to the south and Basford Chemical Works siding and Basford Junction signal-box to the north.

Lincoln Street crossing must have caused considerable hold-ups on the B6004 in the 1950s and 1960s. The Leen Valley line was used not only by passenger trains to and from Mansfield but by numerous coal trains from the collieries at Hucknall and Bestwood.

13 January 1997 David Hucknall

A close-up view of Sutton Station signal-box. Sutton is on the Kirkby to Mansfield section of what had been the Midland Railway's Nottingham and Mansfield Line. Climbing gently from Nottingham to Hucknall via Lenton North Junction, Radford Junction and Bulwell, the line used to climb increasingly steeply towards Annesley before levelling off at Kirkby summit and slipping down towards Sutton and Mansfield.

Opened on 18 September 1910 as a replacement for Sutton Junction North signal-box of April 1893, Sutton station signal-box (so named in February 1960) is slowly but surely declining structurally since its closure in October 1995. A typical Midland Type 4a design, it is very similar to the 'box at Lincoln Street Crossing in Basford (*The Signal-Box*, p. 143). In both cases, the locking-room windows are four panes wide and the entrance end elevations show great similarity. Still visible on the lower vertical boarding at the working level are the blocks to which the original name would have been attached.

24 May 1996 David Hucknall

A close-up of Shirebrook station signal-box. Water leakage has obviously been a problem on the ridge facing the camera. On the landing at the top of the stairs is a backless chair, perhaps to help the signal staff while away the warm, sunny hours waiting for a train.

South of Shirebrook, the line is controlled by Kirkby Summit signal-box, which is now a series of prefabricated cabins.

May 1996 David Hucknall

The remains of the former Shirebrook West station can clearly be seen in this photograph, taken from the road bridge that leads into Shirebrook. In the distance is Shirebrook station signal-box, a Midland Railway Type 2a of 1890. Beyond the 'box is the characteristic shape, instantly recognisable to anyone familiar with coal-mining areas, of a former colliery spoilheap. In this case it was Shirebrook Colliery and the station signal-box once controlled the branch to its yard and sidings.

From this distance, the 'box appears to be in reasonably good condition but, close up, its 106 years are beginning to show.

May 1996 David Hucknall

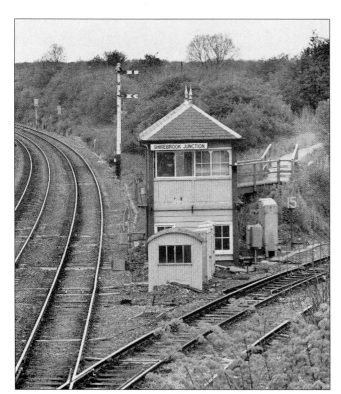

Shirebrook is a small town in the former Derbyshire coalfield. The first railway to arrive there was the Midland, extending its line northwards from Mansfield. Next came the Lancashire, Derbyshire and East Coast Railways. Its line from Lincoln crossed the Midland's north of the latter's station. In 1899, a south-to-east spur was built at Shirebrook Junction, linking the Midland Railway with the LD and ECR at Warsop Junction. In 1904, a further connection was made at Shirebrook Junction (later named Shirebrook North (for Langwith) by the Great Central Railway).

Shirebrook Junction still exists. Its fine, ex-Midland Railway signal-box, dating back to 1899, continues to guard the tracks leading to Warsop Junction and to Shirebrook East Junction but many of the inter-colliery coal trains and all of the excursion traffic has gone. The former MR station is closed, its buildings decaying and its yard used as a parking area for Railtrack vehicles.

David Hucknall

The distinctive Midland Railway signal-box at Pinxton. If one knows where to look, the 'box can be clearly seen, away in the valley, from the northbound M1 between junctions 27 and 28.

The present Pinxton 'box was opened on 24 January 1897 as a replacement for an earlier structure possibly dating from 1875. It lies close to the site of the former Pinxton and Selston station, which was opened in November 1851 and closed to passengers on 16 June 1947.

Pinxton has had a noteworthy railway history. It lay on the Mansfield and Pinxton Railway, built partly to serve the Cromford Canal basin at Pinxton but mainly because the inhabitants of Mansfield wanted better communication with the outside world and wider markets for the town's products. The involvement of the Midland Railway started in about 1845 and an Act was passed on 8 July authorizing that company to purchase the whole of the M&PR line.

Although the track was relaid for steam-train operation in 1847 and later deviations from the original were made, Pinxton signal-box is on a stretch of line that follows closely the course of the old M&PR.

17 June 1994 David Hucknall

The signal-box at Longbridge East is a superb example of an ex-Midland Railway structure. This view was taken from inside the Rover works with the kind cooperation of its security personnel. The 'box was opened on 12 November 1916 as Longbridge, to be renamed Longbridge East on 15 April 1917. It stands close to the remains of the former Longbridge, Halesowen and Old Hill branch, the Halesowen–Halesowen Junction stretch of which opened to goods and passengers on 10 September 1883. The branch was worked jointly by the Midland and GWR under an agreement made in 1872. A relatively short (about 6 miles) branch in its heyday, it ran from Halesowen Junction to Old Hill on the Stourbridge Junction–Snow Hill line. Its activities 40 years ago were reviewed by S.L. Jacobs (*Trains Illustrated*, II, (120), 474 (1958)) who commented, 'Any branch that can boast seven different methods of signalling in the five boxes along its length is unusual to say the least'.

Of the Longbridge East 'box, Jacobs said, 'This box is the key to the rail transport system of the Austin factories and probably handles more movements of Austin locomotives than of B.R. engines, which are themselves considerable'. The Halesowen branch was severed at a point between bridge no. 1 and Longbridge East on 16 July 1965. The Halesowen Junction to Longbridge East line was made a siding on 7 September 1969.

2 June 1996 David Hucknall

In this photograph, taken in the early 1960s from the window of a train on the down former LNWR line to Peterborough, Market Harborough no. 2 signal-box can be seen. This signal-box, together with MH no. 3, were built by the LMSR as replacements for old MR and LNWR cabins. They worked the station and LMS connections to the North. In front of the signal-box, the exchange sidings' double slips can be seen. The bridge in the background leads to the former Midland Railway goods yard in which the 5-ton crane is in action.

Passenger services to Northampton ended in 1960 and the Peterborough–Rugby line closed in 1966, leaving only the former MR Leicester–Bedford route. After the closures, the layout was greatly simplified and worked by no. 2 cabin.

Lawrence James

While taking photographs for this book, I have encountered a few surprising remnants of Britain's railway history. One which particularly delighted me was the nameboard on the signal-box at Northenden Junction on the Glazebrook to Godley Junction section of the Cheshire Lines Railway. I saw it one evening in October 1996. The board is cream on brown with a characteristic style of lettering. I feel sure it is original.

David Hucknall

A close-up of Plumley West signal-box, situated some 1,500 yards from Plumley station on the Lostock Gralam side of Knutsford–Northwich line. It stands near the site of the former ICI Holford Moss chemical plant and the access road is now mainly used by dog walkers.

A 26-lever 'box, designated as a CLC Type 2, it was opened in 1908. Built on a panelled brick baše and having a gabled roof with windows two panes by two panes set at both ends, it has features common to all post-1904 CLR 'boxes. Unusually, however, for a structure built after 1906, it has operating floor windows three panes deep.

8 September 1996 David Hucknall

The distant signal at the end of the Down platform at Plumley station. Opened in 1863 by the Cheshire Midland Railway, the station stands on the Knutsford–Northwich section of the former Cheshire Lines Railway. It is a curious place. It appears to be disused and partly boarded up, although the steps down to the platform and painted platform edges indicate otherwise. The milepost gives the distance from the former Manchester Central station.

The main building remains intact but abandoned. It is decorated with unusual chequered bands of black and white bricks and a large finial leans crookedly at the gable end of the roof. Once 'immaculately kept' (N. Dyckhoff. *The Cheshire Lines Committee – Then and Now*, Ian Allan, 1984), the station even had its own signal-box at the opposite end of the platform as well as facilities for handling goods and livestock. The signal-box closed in 1985 when the stationmaster left. Plumley West signal-box, approximately 1,500 yards further down the track, now controls the line as far as Knutsford.

8 September 1996 David Hucknall

NORTH EASTERN REGION

The North Eastern Region of British Railways and its successors coincided closely with the geographical area served by the North Eastern Railway. Its southern boundary followed the north side of the Humber as far as Goole and headed north-west towards Selby and Leeds. Its western boundary went along the edge of the Pennines, parallel to the Northallerton–Darlington–Durham–Newcastle line. Its eastern boundary was the coastline of the counties of Yorkshire, Durham and Northumberland. while its northern boundary was the Scottish Border. Apart from minimal competition in the south where the NER encountered the Lancashire and Yorkshire railway and the Hull, Barnsley and West Riding Junction Railway, the North Eastern Railway had the monopoly of its territory. It did not, however, abuse its position and provided a good service to its users.

From the point of view of signalling, the North Eastern Railway was initially divided into three divisions – Northern, Central and Southern. Each was responsible for its own signalling and used contractors to build 'boxes to that division's design. The Central division was abolished in 1899 but examples of its signal-boxes still remain.

The present chapter deals predominantly with the 'boxes in the former southern division. One or two examples from the central division are also included but space does not allow coverage of the northern division. The area included now comes under the control of the London North Eastern zone of Railtrack. The East Coast main line passes along the western side of the territory linking Doncaster, York and Newcastle. This line is now supervised by the integrated electronic control centres at York and Doncaster, with the Tyneside IECC taking care of the northern end. Other routes serve the cities such as Leeds, Hull and York and cover a region with lines between Leeds, Selby and Hull, Hull and Scarborough, Scarborough and Leeds, Scarborough and York, and York and Leeds.

A significant part of the subsidiary lines in the area continues to be worked using the absolute block (AB) signalling system. This method was gradually introduced by the railway companies during the latter half of the nineteenth century, although it was not until the mid- to late 1890s that rail passengers could be confident that it was in use throughout Britain. The AB method allows only one train to occupy a track section at any one time. Permission for another train to enter the section is only given when the previous train has left. AB working is found, for example, on sections of the Hull–Selby line (one between Melton Lane and Broomfleet and two between Gilberdyke Junction and Hemingborough). The Scarborough–York line has seven AB sections between Falsgrave and Strensall. The York–Leeds line has AB between Hammerton and Cattall and Knareborough and Horsforth. With the AB system, inter-'box communication is normally by block instruments and some fine, well cared for equipment can be found in 'boxes in the area.

The former southern division signal-boxes fall into four general categories. Type S1 (classification as stated in *The Signal-Box*, 1986) can be found at Castleford station and Selby, for example. A variant, the Type S1a, is widespread and can be found at several locations including Bridlington South, Howden, Kirkham Abbey, Peckfield and Thorpe Gates. The S1bs were small, low- or ground-level 'boxes. Howsham is a typical example. S2b 'boxes are only found on the main line out of Hull with one example on the Doncaster branch. Six examples are currently in use, including the signal-boxes at Brough East, Cave, Cayton, Goole and Seamer East and West. McKenzie and Holland dominated southern division signalling from the 1870s to almost the 1920s.

In conclusion, two fascinating examples of non-standard 'boxes may also be found in the southern area. Goole Swing Bridge signal-box, dating from 1869, is the oldest signal-box in Britain. It controls both river and rail traffic. The 'box on the swing-bridge over the River Ouse at Selby fulfills a similar task. Once, all rail traffic on the East Coast main line going to and from York, passed over the bridge. It sees a mere fraction of that nowadays.

Semaphore signalling can still be found in the region. Invariably, it is the ubiquitous steel-posted upper quadrant type. The North Eastern Railway, however, had very elegant signals with tall 'half ball and spike' finials. An interesting contrast can be made in this chapter between the fine ex-NER bracket signal at Peckfield in the 1960s and the functional bracket signals at Seamer West or Castleford station in the 1990s.

Class A3 Pacific no. 60073 *St. Gatien* of Heaton shed enters Durham station with the 9.00 a.m. Liverpool–Newcastle train on 27 September 1961. Behind the locomotive is a former North Eastern Railway signal gantry carrying both NER lower quadrant signals and LNER upper quadrants.

The smaller signals on the gantry are subsidiary signals to control shunting and other movements within the station. The miniature signals mounted below the main running line stop signals are for shunting movements on running lines in the same direction as the normal flow of through traffic (Kitchenside and Williams. *British Railway Signalling*, 4th ed., Ian Allan, 1978, p. 22). For example, shunt-ahead arms allow a train to draw forward into the block section ahead before reversing into a siding or loop.

David Holmes

Selby swing-bridge, with its signal-box/control cabin, provides a rail crossing over the Yorkshire Ouse. The river at this point is tidal and often used by sea-going vessels and general traffic. The 130-foot structure was opened in 1891 with the obviously non-standard cabin astride the tracks which, until October 1983, carried East Coast main line trains on their way between York and Doncaster.

Up to 1960, relatively few changes were made to the bridge. During that year, however, the track on the bridge was replaced and colour-light signalling was installed in place of semaphores. This allowed the intricate equipment, by which the wires to the signals on the north side of the river were connected and disconnected on the opening and closing of the bridge, to be dismantled. The cabin was also raised by 3 ft 6 ins.

9 July 1996 David Hucknall

The sight of any former Western Region steam locomotive would have been highly unusual in the north-east of England. In the late summer of 1967, however, 'Castle' class 4–6–0 no. 7029 *Clun Castle* was involved in clearance trials at Newcastle-upon-Tyne station.

Here, 7029 is seen passing through Gateshead heading towards the King Edward Bridge. Colour-light signals G145 and G146 dominate the picture and are controlled by Gateshead power signal-box. This 'box was opened in 1963 when it took over work previously carried out by cabins at Bensham Curve, King Edward Bridge, Greensfield, High Street and Park Lane.

David Hucknall

The railway came to Goole in 1848 when the Lancashire and Yorkshire Railway made the town its eastern terminus. The NER arrived much later, in 1863, with a line from Doncaster.

The signal-box at Goole lies immediately south-west of the station on the level-crossing of the A614/A151 with the railway. Opened in 1909, Goole signal-box was formerly known as Boothferry Road (Booth Ferry House lay to the north-north-west, close to where the A614 crosses the River Ouse). It is a good example of a North Eastern Railway Type S4 with a concrete band at the operating floor level and concrete lintels over the locking-frame windows (now bricked up). The windows are four panes deep and the 'box is glazed on all sides for good visibility. An interesting feature of the S4 'box was the relatively plain bargeboards having part-circular ends.

17 February 1996 David Hucknall

The signal-box on the swing-bridge over the River Ouse, two miles north-east of Goole. This signal-box, built by the North Eastern Railway in 1869, is the oldest operational 'box on Britain's railways.

Requests to open the swing-bridge are received in the 'box by radio from the river pilot on ships approaching the bridge. In December 1973, Goole Bridge was put out of action for eight months after a German coaster hit one of the fixed spans.

17 February 1996 David Hucknall

The former North Eastern Railway signal-box at Brough East. The 'box, which was opened on 28 February 1904, is a southern division Type 2, one of several which were unique to the Hull district of that railway (M. Nicholson. *The Signalling Record,* (59), Sept./Oct. 1996, p. 149). There were sixteen S2 boxes on the line between Hull Paragon and Staddlethorpe Junction (Gilberdyke) but now only four remain.

The NER S2 'boxes were designed to have fixed dimensions − 12 ft wide and 8 ft 6 ins above rail level − although there were some variations in length and, in the case of a gate 'box such as Cave Crossing, height variations also.

18 February 1996 David Hucknall

Signalman Frank Taylor watches the road out of the window of the level-crossing 'box at Cave. Behind him is the wheel that operates the barriers and some of the 16 levers of the McKenzie and Holland frame. An old armchair and a bottle of squash are fairly basic comforts for a long stint on duty.

David Hucknall

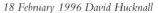

The gate 'box at Cave in East Yorkshire was opened by the North Eastern Railway in 1904. Through one of the windows on the right-hand side can be seen the signalman, Frank Taylor.

The weather at the start of 1996 was treacherous and, during the previous week, Mr Taylor had been driving to work only to become stuck in a snowdrift yards from the 'box.

18 February 1996 David Hucknall

Broomfleet signal-box, on the Hull–Gilberdyke section of the former NER main line in east Yorkshire, is a further example of a NER Type S2 'box. It was opened on 19 May 1904 and remains in operation with Cave and Gilberdyke. Very much the standard S2 (12 ft wide, 8 ft 6 ins high) it has certain features which are no longer present on Brough East 'box. These are the locking-room windows, which are cast iron with semi-circular tops.

18 February 1996 David Hucknall

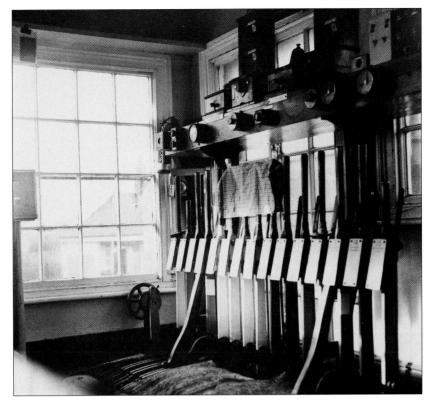

The inside of the signal-box at Howden. On the block shelf, the instruments are labelled with the names of the 'boxes working with Howden–Hemingbrough to the west and Gilberdyke to the east.

The level-crossing near Howden 'box is operated from the control box on the left-hand side of the photograph and the signal-wire tensioning wheel is in front of the window, close to the signal frame. Some rudimentary protection from draughts is provided by the piece of matting covering the central lever slots. A tea towel is drying on the handles of the redundant levers on the frame.

February 1996 David Hucknall

Howden is a very pleasant little town in south Yorkshire and once had two stations. The one at the northern edge of the town was opened by the Hull, Barnsley and West Riding Junction Railway in July 1885. It was closed on 1 August 1955. The other station, over a mile from Howden on the B1228, still exists. It was opened on 1 July 1840 by the Hull and Selby Railway as Howden and Bubwith (although Bubwith is some 5½ miles from the station). Renamed and renamed yet again, it became Howden in 1961.

The line on which Howden stands is the longest straight length of track in Britain. For 18 miles, the railway travels across the flat land from Hemingbrough without the slightest curve until just before East Ferriby. The signal-box is a North Eastern Railway Type S1a, opened in about 1873. It contains a 16-lever McKenzie and Holland frame (see plate above) fitted in 1905 and controls the crossing of the railway by the B1228. It works in conjunction with the 'boxes at Hemingbrough and Gilberdyke.

David Hucknall

The signal-box at Peckfield and a tall, rather elegant balanced bracket signal are shown in this photograph. Peckfield signal-box stood opposite Peckfield Colliery by the side of the former NER line from Leeds to York/Selby.

The two distant signals seen here were worked by Micklefield signal-box (the pit village of New Micklefield can be seen in the distance) where the routes diverge. The upper quadrant distant for the York direction is 'off'. The lower quadrant home and distant signals are for the Selby line.

Many years ago, the old Great North Road passed under the railway line at New Micklefield and snaked through Old Micklefield towards Aberford. The present A1 roars over the railway, by-passing the Micklefields. Peckfield colliery may have long gone but Micklefield station and signal-box remain.

David Holmes

I had not intended to take the A63 out of Selby to get to Church Fenton. It was an unexpected pleasure, therefore, to come across Thorpe Gates signal-box. It is situated on the flat land between Selby and South Milford near Thorpe Willoughby, where the former Leeds and Selby line of the North Eastern Railway crosses the A63.

An NER Southern Division Type 1a 'box dating back to about 1873, it has been altered both internally and externally. Inside, individual function switches were fitted in 1973. The external alteration is a relatively small extension of the 'box which is clearly visible in this photograph.

9 July 1996 David Hucknall

Selby signal-box is on the former Leeds–Selby line. It carries both its present name and its previous name 'Selby West'. The 'box has undergone several changes of name since its opening in 1870. Originally named 'London Road', it then became Wistow Junction. Wistow was on the single line to Cawood that diverged from the Leeds–Selby route in the vicinity of the 'box.

Selby signal-box has also undergone significant structural alteration. It was originally a North Eastern Railway Southern Division Type 1 but was extended in 1904. It varies from the standard S1 design by having a hipped roof; reroofing may have occurred during its extension (*The Signal-Box*, 1986). It has, however, retained the three-panes-deep operating floor windows always found on Type 1 structures.

9 July 1996 David Hucknall

Church Fenton station lies approximately 10¾ miles south of York on the former LNER lines between York and Leeds and York and Burton Salmon. It has known much better days. When this photograph was taken the station was deserted, a far cry from the days when its four platforms would have served the nearby and important RAF Church Fenton.

Photographed from the north end of the station, Church Fenton signal-box (formerly Church Fenton North) overlooks the convergence of the lines from Sherburn in Elmet and the south (tracks on the right) and those from Micklefield and Leeds (on the left).

9 July 1996 David Hucknall

Taken from the edge of the 'PYO' fruit field just north of the station, this closer view of Church Fenton signal-box reveals some interesting details. The 'box is a North Eastern Railway Type S3, a design found mainly on the line between York and Burton Salmon, and was opened in 1904. The bargeboards are relatively plain yet have trefoils cut out at the head and foot. A notable feature of the S3s was said to be large (two panes deep) upper lights above the operating floor windows. These are boarded up at Church Fenton. An extended brick/concrete base and a dominant chimney are also unusual. The woodwork of the 'box is now painted a rather odd dark red/brown colour.

9 July 1996 David Hucknall

Poppleton station is approximately 3 miles from York on the York, Knaresborough and Harrogate branch. This begins at Skelton Junction on the East Coast main line, about 1¾ miles north of York and turns away to the west. Once off the main line, the gradient increases from almost level to 1 in 352 and then 1 in 284 before Poppleton.

The branch was once double line with nine stations but four, including Hessay and Marston Moor, were closed to passengers in September 1958. Poppleton station is very well kept. It has a small signal cabin, said to be an NER Southern Division Type 1 dating from the 1870s, which controls the adjacent level-crossing. At Poppleton the double line continues as single track as far as Hammerton and in this photograph Railtrack personnel are ultrasonically testing the track in use.

9 July 1996 David Hucknall

Knaresborough is on the 20½-mile route between York and Harrogate. At the approach to the station, the line enters a deep cutting and a tunnel, then it emerges into the station which is cut into the hillside.

There is a small stone-built signal-box at Knaresborough, built by the North Eastern Railway and opened in about 1870. This photograph shows the 'box at the end of a terrace of stone houses descending a steep hill.

1 October 1995 David Hucknall

Starbeck station stands on the York–Knaresborough–Harrogate line. At the southern end of the station there is a passenger subway connecting the platforms. Pictured here is the signal-box at Starbeck. Originally a North Eastern Railway Southern Division Type 1a 'box, it controls the level-crossing on the A59 between Harrogate and York.

The approach to Harrogate from York via Starbeck is relatively steep. On leaving Knaresborough, the line crosses the River Nidd and climbs at 1 in 105 for almost a mile before turning sharply right at 1 in 142 into Starbeck. In steam days, it would have passed the goods yard and Starbeck's m.p.d. Between the station and the site of the former North Junction, the gradient is considerably easier (1 in 426/212) but steepens to 1 in 82/104 on the former Dragon loop before the final climb to Harrogate.

17 May 1996 David Hucknall

YORK–SCARBOROUGH

This photograph shows the 'tapper' and bell on the block shelf at Seamer East signal-box used to communicate with Seamer West. The brass identification plate below the instrument is brightly polished, showing the respect with which most signalmen regard railway history.

David Hucknall

The instrument shelf, signal frame and levers inside Seamer East signal-box are shown in this photograph. The frame is marked 'McKenzie & Holland, Worcester'. Starting from the entrance-end of the 'box, the levers visible are numbered 1–5, 6, 7, 8, 9, 10, 36, 11, 14, 15. Of these, numbers 6, 7, 9 and 10 are further labelled: no. 6, Down Main Distants (7, 9, 10); no. 7, Down Main First Home for interlocking purposes only; no. 9, Down Main Home; no. 10, Down Main Starter (Line Clear).

David Hucknall

Throughout the country, from Newhaven to Settle Junction, no opportunity ever seems to be missed by signalling staff to make their surroundings as pleasant as possible. At their own expense, window-boxes are planted to disguise uninteresting walls and hanging baskets are arranged to brighten dull corners and hide peeling paintwork.

At Seamer East, for example, the embankment behind two disused sidings has been planted and embellished with plaster gnomes. Standing at the top of the stairs to the 'box is the 'gardener' who, although retired, continues to beautify Seamer station and its signal-box. He used to look after the displays at Filey and Scarborough as well but this is now not possible because, by some administrative oversight, he can no longer obtain free rail travel to reach them.

25 August 1996 David Hucknall

Seamer West signal-box lies about half a mile to the south-west of Seamer station, close to Seamer Junction. Three routes once came together at the junction – the single-line Pickering and Scarborough branch (now closed) and the York and Scarborough, and Hull and Scarborough branches. In this distant view of Seamer West, the junction signal for the diverging routes to Hull (left-hand signal) and York dominates the picture. The separate signals for the converging routes can also be seen behind the 'box.

From the beginning of this century to the outbreak of the First World War, a little-known express (known as 'The Leeds Flyer') ran during summer services and covered the 67½ miles from Scarborough to Leeds in 75 minutes (G.W.G. Cass. *The Stephenson Locomotive Society Journal*, 32 (371), 116 (1956)). This would have been a quicker journey but for speed restrictions between Seamer and Seamer Junction. Once clear of the junction, it would dash along at 70 m.p.h. to Malton, which could be reached in 20 minutes from Scarborough.

David Hucknall

On its way between York and Scarborough, the former York and Scarborough Branch of the NER is skirting the 75-ft contour over the level-crossing at Howsham. Northbound, it is also following a sweeping bend on the River Derwent. It next crosses a small road which leads to Kirkham Priory and Castle Howard.

Photographed from the level-crossing, Kirkham signal-box and the crossing gates can be seen at the end of the platform of the now closed Kirkham Abbey station. In the background, the road curves away behind the station and climbs up the wooded hillside.

One of Yorkshire's ubiquitous NER Type S1a 'boxes, it dates from 1873 and has a 16-lever reconditioned McKenzie and Holland frame installed in 1926.

August 1996 David Hucknall

A photograph showing a side elevation of the upper half of the gate-box at Howsham on the York–Scarborough line. In front of the 'box, part of the crossing gate with its warning lamp can be seen barring the road (see accompanying photograph). In the valley between the 'box and the hill, the River Derwent flows, meandering towards the River Ouse.

Howsham 'box was opened in about 1873 (*The Signal-Box Directory*, 1992). It is a former North Eastern Railway Southern Division Type 1b, and uses a 9-lever McKenzie and Holland frame which was fitted in 1891.

25 August 1996 David Hucknall

A horse and rider stand at the crossing at Howsham. The gate-box (a former NER Type S1b) was opened in 1873 but the present 9-lever frame was brought into operation in 1891. It lies on the former York and Scarborough line of the NER which, at that point, follows a bend in the River Derwent that begins at Kirkham. The road down to the crossing is relatively insignificant, gently descending into the river valley towards Barton le Willows and Howsham, passing by Crambe village as it does so.

Normally, the crossing gates are closed with the railway signals off and the gate-box unmanned. Operation of the push button, shown in the photograph, alerts the gate operator who is called from a nearby house. Although the gates are manually operated, the signals must be returned to the 'on' position by the operator using levers inside the 'box.

25 August 1996 David Hucknall

A view of the signal-box at Beverley station. Beverley station was an example of G.T. Andrews' 'train sheds'. He was the architect for the York and North Midlands Railway and designed the contemporary stations at Bridlington and Great Driffield.

In LNER days, the line branched just north of Beverley to York and Market Weighton and the Hull and Scarborough line continued northward to Driffield where it was joined by the Malton and Driffield and the Scarborough and Selby lines.

The signal-box dates from 1911 and is a NER Southern Division Type 4. It is fitted with a McKenzie and Holland Type 16 frame, which is now reduced to 20 levers.

25 August 1996 David Hucknall

Cayton station was on the Hull and Scarborough line of the NER and its successor the LNER. It was opened by the York and North Midland Railway on 5 October 1846 and finally closed in May 1952. It was located about half a mile south of Cayton village on the road to Folkton.

Very little remains of the station now. What had been a platform is just a level grassy area, slightly raised, by the side of the single track. The gate-box at Cayton continues to be operational. A former NER Type S4 of 1908, it was fitted with a second-hand McKenzie and Holland frame dating from 1886. The crossing continues to be manned, the gatekeeper living in a house behind the signal-box.

On receiving a bell signal from either Filey or Seamer West, the gatekeeper will close the gates and operate the appropriate signal levers.

August 1996 David Hucknall

Bridlington South signal-box, seen from the end of no. 6 platform of the station, looks a handsome structure. Even on a summer Sunday, however, the station was empty and forgotten. Its redundant platforms were a sad reminder of the great popularity of 'Brid' as a seaside resort for many people from the West Riding of Yorkshire over a large number of years. The large trackless areas of land around the station are evidence of the once-extensive carriage sidings at the southern end of the station.

The signal-box, originally named Bridlington station, is a North Eastern Railway Southern Division Type 1a. In 1912, as a result of a significant increase in rail traffic, it was extended and a 125-lever frame fitted. As the decline set in, there was less need for railway facilities. Bridlington's motive power depot, where excursion locomotives were serviced, closed in 1958. The frame in the signal-box was reduced to 65 levers in 1974. similar changes took place at Quay Crossing signal-box at the eastern end of the station.

25 August 1996 David Hucknall

A touch of domesticity at Cayton gate 'box – seen through the windows is a large, shiny kettle on a 'Baby Belling' hotplate. On the lovely late August morning when this photograph was taken, with shadows of the clouds drifting over the river valley and Folkton Brow and Flixton Wold, these items seem a little irrelevant but when winter snows grip East Yorkshire, they are essential.

Reflected in the windows are the branches of the yew tree that has stood close to the 'box for many years. The gate-operator's husband told me that in early photographs of Cayton station and its staff, this tree also figured prominently.

David Hucknall

Hunmanby station is on the 'coastal' route between Bridlington and Scarborough. It is approximately 3 miles south-south-west of Filey on the flattish uplands that rise behind Filey Bay. The station is at the south-eastern corner of Hunmanby and the signal-box (a NER Type S1a of 1875) stands at the end of the Scarborough-bound platform, overseeing the level-crossing. The crossing gates are of 'traditional' appearance, each gate carrying a semi-circular warning plate.

25 August 1996 David Hucknall

Bedale was on the Wensleydale line that once ran for 22 miles from Castle Hills Junction, just north of Northallerton to Garsdale. Opened on 1 February 1855, Bedale used to be 'one of the prettiest stations on the Wensleydale branch' having a single platform with 'fine floral displays' (S.C. Jenkins. *The Wensleydale Branch: A New History*, The Oakwood Press, 1993, p. 96).

To the west of Bedale station, there is a level-crossing on the road to Leyburn. Bedale signal-box used to be a handsome structure, built in the NER Southern Division style. It had 31 levers which controlled home, starting and shunting signals. For many years, the signals were of typical North Eastern Railway lower quadrant, slotted post type. They were later replaced by standard upper quadrant British Railway semaphores.

Seen in mid-May 1996, the boarded-up, 120-year-old signal-box is gradually decaying. The single track, ending at Leyburn, still exists – weed-covered, with shaky sleepers and little ballast. It is now used, very rarely, by the Army.

David Hucknall

Urlay Nook is on a minor road leading from the A66 at Long Newton to the A67 in the south. The road crosses the railway line between Stockton and Darlington. The signal-box oversees the crossing and looks out onto a chemical works which produces chromium compounds.

A former North Eastern Railway Type C2a (C representing the Central Division) 'box of about 1896, Urlay Nook belies its 100 years. The brickwork is well-pointed and the roof is sound.

Compared to the crossing gates and barriers seen in other areas, those found in certain parts of the former North Eastern region of British Railways are unusual. Known as boom gates, they have the slightly eccentric appearance of a red-and-white-painted fence. The rubber-tyred wheels powered by a direct-drive electric motor ensure their smooth operation.

17 May 1996 David Hucknall

Heighington station is on the former LNER Bishop Auckland and Darlington branch, which crossed Great Aycliffe before heading north-west at School Aycliffe towards Shildon and Bishop Auckland. The station is approximately 1½ miles east of Heighington village in an area now dominated by the micro-electronics industry. The Up and Down platforms are unusual, being separated by a level-crossing, and the platform shelters have fading murals depicting the long railway history of the region.

The signal-box at Heighington is much older than its appearance seems to suggest. According to *The Signal-Box Directory* (1992), it dates from about 1872 and is a former NER Central Division Type 1a. Allen and Wolstenholmes suggest that the basic design may be taken from one by the Stockton and Darlington Railway. They note that the 'magnificent bargeboards with intersecting cross timbers and finials over six feet long' and a tall chimney are not present.

3 October 1995 David Hucknall

Whitby station was designed by G.T. Andrews and opened in 1847. At the end of no. 4 platform was a goods warehouse. The 1884 North Eastern Railway 'box, shown in this photograph, adjoined the warehouse. To give the signalman a view over the roof of this shed, the operating floor of the brick-built 'box was one storey higher than usual.

As originally built, the signal-box had an external staircase to the first floor but an internal one to the higher level. When the frame was extended, this layout was altered to the one shown.

Lawrence James

Castleford station signal-box is a North Eastern Railway Southern Division Type 1 opened in 1882. David Holmes, who has provided a number of photographs in this book, was appointed stationmaster at Castleford in March 1968. He was in charge of a large and busy area with two passenger stations, thirteen signal-boxes, eight collieries, a coking plant, a glass works and two chemical works. The post of stationmaster ceased to exist at the end of January 1970.

The 'box appeared to be in reasonable condition when this photograph was taken. Just beyond the station is Castleford West Junction and the line passing behind the 'box leads to Pontefract Monkhill and Knottingley. Castleford station, Methley junction, Altofts Junction and Whitwood Junction 'boxes closed at the end of September 1997.

22 February 1995 David Hucknall

A left-hand bracket signal at Castleford station. The main stem of the signal consists of steel channels with plates welded between as spacers. The signal posts are of a standard design, made of tubular steel. On each post, there is a single man-landing for work on the top signal arm.

Attached to the lower right-hand side of the main support is a post which must have been fitted with a miniature signal arm, possibly controlling a loop line or siding on the right-hand side of the existing track. The signal gantries were removed in September 1997.

February 1995 David Hucknall

SOUTHERN REGION

The area covered by this chapter is restricted to the territory formerly served by the London South Western Railway and the London Brighton and South Coast Railway. The LSWR and the LBSCR, together with the SECR, were the consitutent companies forming the Southern Railway under the 1921 Railways Act. In the 1960s and 1970s, the successor to the Southern Railway, the Southern Region of British Railways, intended to eliminate all mechanical and manual signal-boxes and control its territory from seven major power signal-boxes. This was not achieved and in the South Western division alone, over thirty signal-boxes are still used to control rail traffic. Taken together with the 'boxes on the Central Division (Dorking to Arundel and Hastings to Lewes, Chichester and Havant), some superb examples of the work of the LSWR, the LBSCR and its contractors and the Southern Railway still exist.

Although widely scattered throughout the region, a reasonable selection of former LSWR 'boxes remains. All the standard designs, from the Type 1 at Crediton to the Type 4 at Haslemere, are represented. On the Bournemouth–Weymouth line, six out of the eight 'boxes originated with the LSWR. Bournemouth Carriage Sidings Ground frame (as the former West Junction 'box is now known) is a superb example of a LSWR Type 3a 'box. Apart from the staircase, it appears to be in its original state with the vertical boarding, upper lights and a large wooden roof ventilator. A careful reproduction of the original name, 'West Junction', was fitted by a previous manager in connection with the depot's centenary celebrations. Inside, the Stevens' frame still has its levers with plates fitted close to their bases as in LSWR days.

The LBSCR is also well represented in the list of remaining signal-boxes to be found on the former Southern region. Saxby and Farmer had the monopoly of the LBSCR's signal work. Examples of their Type 5 'box, introduced in 1876 and widely regarded as one of the most stylish signal-box designs ever built, (*The Signal-Box*, 1986), can be found on the former LBSCR line between Arundel and Dorking (Pulborough, Warnham, Holmwood), the Lewes–Hastings line and the Newhaven branch.

Early in its history, the Southern Railway attached considerable importance to its public image. Sir Herbert Walker appointed John Elliot as assistant for Public Relations in January 1925, the first holder of such a post on a British railway. As its electrification schemes progressed, so the Southern wished to project a more modern image. For example, Wimbledon station was given a new façade in 1929 and the 1930s saw the reconstruction of stations at Surbiton, Horsham, etc. In its signal-boxes, too, the style of the SR was emerging. First introduced at Surbiton in 1936, the design was, and still is, striking. Flat-roofed, with a substantial overhang, the 'boxes were made of brick and concrete with rounded corners at the operating floor level. With the large plate-glass windows and sometimes subtle decorations on the side walls, these 'boxes have 'style'. Examples are widespread – Dorking, Bognor, Templecombe – they all remain eye-catching. Even when no longer working and 'tagged', as with Wimbledon 'A', they dominate and impress.

The constituent companies of the Southern railway used semaphore signalling and, in some cases, their approach was innovative. On the main line between Woking and Basingstoke, for example, the LSWR installed automatic, pneumatically actuated lower quadrant signals. These impressive structures remained in place until 1967. Usually, however, signalling changes in the region were brought about in the 1920s and 1930s in connection with the spread of electrification. For example, from March 1926, three and four aspect colour-light signalling was in use on the line between Holborn Viaduct and Elephant and Castle. During the late 1920s and 1930s, the Southern Railway completed its plans for the electrification of its routes in the London suburbs and, in most cases, with it went the semaphores.

Nowadays, it is relatively difficult to find semaphore signals on the former Southern Region. One must travel the lines between Dorking and Arundel or Hastings and Lewes. Without a doubt, however, the best location is along the Fawley–Totton line on the west side of Southampton Water. There, examples of finialled, lattice-post, upper quadrant bracket signals, so reminiscent of the days of the Southern Railway, can be found.

The balanced bracket, splitting stop signal shown in this photograph is at Marchwood on the Fawley branch. The former LSWR lattice-post signal is fitted with later SR upper quadrant arms. The finials are typical of Saxby & Farmer.

David Hucknall

SOUTHAMPTON–WAREHAM

Signal levers inside Bournemouth Carriage Sidings Ground Frame.

2 May 1997 David Hucknall

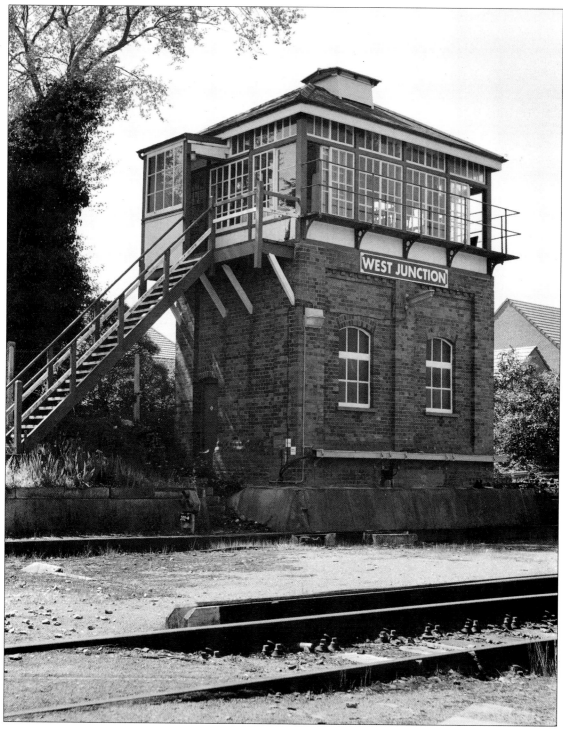

The signal-box now known as Bournemouth Carriage Sidings Ground Frame is very rarely photographed. It stands at the side of the inward road at the entrance to Bournemouth Traction and Rolling Stock Maintenance Depot. This is close to the point where the lines between Bournemouth West and Bournemouth Central stations once joined the Branksome–Bournemouth West branch; A triangular junction was formed with the Branksome–Bournemouth Central line.

The 'box is a delight to see. It is a London South Western Railway Type 3a cabin opened in 1888. Painted in green and cream, it still carries an enamel nameboard, also in green and white, bearing its original name 'West Junction'. There is a 24-lever Stevens' frame inside the cabin on which only 10 levers are in use.

2 May 1997 David Hucknall

119

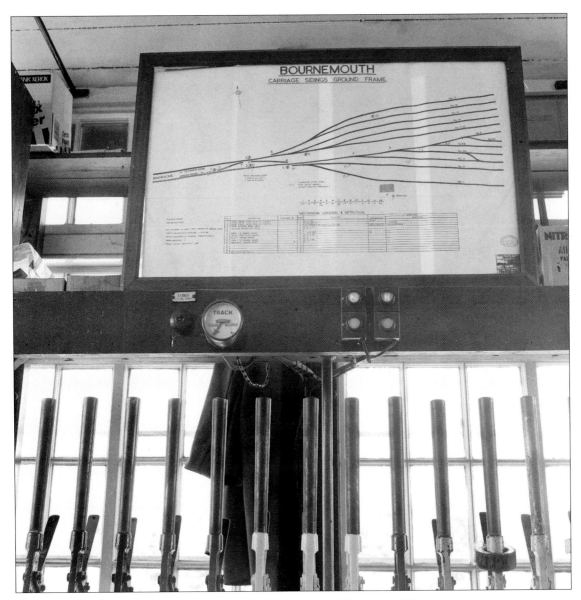

Track diagram and signal lever handles inside Bournemouth Carriage sidings ground frame.

2 May 1997 David Hucknall

Branksome station is on the main line between Poole and Bournemouth. Only the rented station buildings at road level detract from a surprisingly clean, pleasant and intact station. Branksome signal-box is situated at the end of the Up platform. Here, the branch to the Bournemouth Traction and Rolling Stock Maintenance Depot curves away to the south-east. This line used to lead to Bournemouth West Junction and then Bournemouth West Station (closed in October 1965).

Branksome 'box is said to be an LSWR Type 3a and was opened on 14 December 1886 (G.A. Pryer. 'Signal-box Diagrams of the Great Western and Southern Railways', *SR Lines in East Dorset*, vol. 2, p. 42). Just over 20 ft long and 13 ft 7 ins wide, it has a 30-lever Stevens' frame. It is brick-built with simply-decorated panels. The 'box is also relatively high (14 ft above the ground). Where the present signal WBZ25 stands, a balanced bracket semaphore signal stood. Initially controlling the Up main and Down branch lines, alterations were made in November 1965 when, among others, the Down branch signals were removed.

September 1994 David Hucknall

The first signal-box to the west of Branksome, on the Waterloo–Weymouth line, is Poole. The former Poole 'B' 'box, now known only as Poole, was opened by the London, South Western Railway in about 1897. As Poole 'B', it was extended from 27 to the present 51 levers in the mid- to late 1930s following resignalling of the area.

The 'box, an LSWR Type 4, stands approximately 260 yds from the Wareham end of Poole's Down platform, opposite the former goods yard. Seen here in end elevation, the 'box is shown with a Down train passing on its way to Hamworthy and the west. Through the now double-glazed window, the signalman can be seen in the act of sending 'Train Entering Section' to Wareham (Hamworthy Junction is now switched out except for Poole Quay traffic on certain days of the week).

1996 David Hucknall

Wareham signal-box, on the line between Bournemouth, Poole and Dorchester, is a neat, well-kept structure. Built by the Southern Railway, in a style similar to the LSWR Type 4a design, it has a brick base (21 ft 8 ins by 12 ft 7 ins) with the working level just over 8 ft from the ground. Opened on 25 March 1928, it has a 30-lever Tyer's frame (Stevens pattern).

20 May 1995 David Hucknall

Another view of the signal-box at Wareham from the overbridge at the east end of the station. Pedestrians wait for access to the foot crossing as a train to Waterloo accelerates away from its stop.

The original road/rail crossing at Wareham was altered in December 1969 and new wicket gates were provided. The road gates were removed in April 1980 but the wickets remained for pedestrians. In June 1988, the present crossing was opened, protected by the warning lights shown in the photograph.

20 May 1995 David Hucknall

Grateley is approximately 72 miles from Waterloo on the line to Salisbury and Exeter. Now, it is the next station, eastbound, out of Salisbury.

This photograph shows the signal-box at Grateley shortly before its closure on 2 May 1968. Located on the Up platform, it was opened by the London South Western Railway on 20 July 1901 as a replacement for an earlier cabin which had stood on the Down platform. Originally, the 1901 Grateley 'box had a low-pressure pneumatic frame but was converted to mechanical operation in January 1919. The unusual arrangement of working level windows was probably to ensure a good view of the sidings and loading dock — which were located at the ends and behind the Up platform — and their connections to the main lines.

George Harrison/P. Alvey Collection

Porton station was 78.23 miles from Waterloo on the former main line between Worting Junction and Salisbury. At this point, east-bound trains would be climbing out of Salisbury, up Porton bank at 1 in 140, the line generally following the course of the River Bourne.

The former LSWR Porton signal-box was on the Up platform. It controlled a section of the line with Tunnel Junction 'box at Salisbury (4 miles 465 yds to the west) and Grateley 'box (5 miles 964 yds to the east). Between Grateley and Porton, there was another 'box at Allington but, certainly in the early 1960s, this was open only in the summer. On weekdays, Porton signal-box was in use from 5.45 a.m. to 12.00 p.m. Summer Sundays would see it open in the early afternoon (11.30 a.m. to 2.45 p.m.) and evening (5.00 p.m. to 10.15 p.m.).

Porton signal-box finally closed on 2 May 1968.

George Harrison/P. Alvey Collection

Colour-light running signals at Yeovil Junction. Both YJ44 and 42 are three-aspect signals with white light junction indicators. The island platform from which the photograph was taken can be used by trains travelling in either direction and the horizontal indicator on YJ42 refers to the first left-hand divergence.

In the distance, Yeovil Junction signal-box can be seen. Originally, an LSWR Type 4 of 1909, it has undergone considerable alteration. It now has windows similar to those fitted to GW Type 7 'boxes and a 44-lever GW VTS frame, the latter installed in 1967.

31 March 1995 David Hucknall

The signal-box at Gillingham in Dorset stands on the Down side of a loop on the Salisbury–Exeter line. Opened on 28 April 1957, it is a plain but not unattractive structure, described as a British Railways (Southern Region) Type 16 design. It retains its 30-lever Westinghouse A3 frame.

July 1995 David Hucknall

Templecombe (28½ miles west of Salisbury on the line to Exeter) lies about halfway up Templecombe bank, a gradient varying between 1 in 160 and 1 in 80, climbing from the Blackmore Vale to the start of the Yeo Valley.

Before being drastically modified by the Southern Railway in the late 1930s, Templecombe was once described as '. . . about the most depressing and inconvenient station to be found in the South of England' (*The Railway Magazine*, vol. 85, (December 1939), p. 405).

The striking signal-box, opened in 1938 during the rehabilitation, is classified as a SR Type 13 design. With its rounded corners, large square windows and flat, overhanging concrete roof, it is in a style that I find greatly appealing.

May 1997 David Hucknall

Approximately 43 miles from Waterloo, Haslemere is on the Portsmouth direct line of the former London and South Western Railway. Located on the Down main platform, Haslemere signal-box is an excellent example of that railway's Type 4 cabin. Opened in 1895, it has a 47-lever Stevens' (Railway Signalling Co.) frame. Until their closure, Haslemere 'box worked with Witley station 'box (4 miles 934 yds away in the Up direction) and the one at Liphook (3 miles 1,330 yds away in the Down direction) They were closed in February 1975.

David Hucknall

Overlooking the crossing of the A272 by the Portsmouth line, Petersfield signal-box is eye-catching. A LSWR Type 3 'box, probably built between 1884 and 1888, its operating floor is entirely glazed with panels four panes deep and three panes across. Upper lights are almost obscured by a deep valancing.

Petersfield 'box now controls a section some 18 miles long from about 1 mile south of Liphook almost to Havant. Some forty years ago, it worked with Liss station 'box (3 miles 526 yds) to the north and Buriton Sidings 'box (2 miles 726 yards) to the south.

26 December 1996 David Hucknall

With its windows broken and debris piled close to the tracks, the signal-box at Ilfracombe is seen prior to its demolition in this undated photograph. Built by the Southern Railway in about 1924, the 'box is very similar to that at Barnstaple Junction described below. Behind the 'box rises Comyn Hill with Shield Tor further to the right.

The line from Barnstaple Junction to Ilfracombe was approximately 15 miles in length. It opened on 20 July 1874. From midway between Wrafton and Braunton, it climbed at 1 in 40, round curve after curve to Mortehoe before beginning the 3-mile descent at 1 in 36 to Ilfracombe.

The line to Ilfracombe closed to regular passenger trains in October 1970 although the track was not lifted until 1975.

George Harrison/P. Alvey Collection

Barnstaple Junction 'B' signal-box was opened on 23 July 1924. It was a replacement for the original 1874 'box built for the opening of the Barnstaple and Ilfracombe Railway which started from a junction with the North Devon line.

Originally named Barnstaple Junction West signal-box, it was renamed 'B' 'box in 1949. In this photograph the bridges carrying the Sticklepath Road over the lines to Torrington (to the left) and Ilfracombe (foreground) can be seen.

'B' 'box was closed on 21 May 1971 when the line between Barnstaple and Umberleigh was singled and the layout around Barnstaple simplified. The 'A' 'box closed in November 1987.

George Harrison/P. Alvey Collection

Once, Crediton was the major intermediate rail traffic centre between Exeter and Barnstaple. The station originally had two signal-boxes (East and West) which were opened on 2 June 1875. The West 'box handled some eighty trains per day. It was open twenty-four hours a day, seven days a week and was manned by three signalmen on shifts (J. Nicholas. *The North Devon Line*, Sparkford, OPC, 1992).

The former Crediton West 'box, near the minor road between Crediton and Fordton, has seen great changes in rail operations. A LSWR Type 1 pattern 'box (as at Alresford), it originally had 22 levers and a Stevens' frame. The 'box controlled the distant, home, starting and advanced starting signals in both directions, the level-crossing and the pointwork.

Changes began in 1971. A pair of crossovers to the west of the level-crossing were installed, making Crediton a junction. What had been the Up and Down lines to Exeter then became separate lines – one to Meldon and one to Barnstaple. The level-crossing was converted to lifting barriers in January 1974 and, on 16 December 1984, the old 'box was equipped with a colour-light signalling panel.

21 August 1994 David Hucknall

Marchwood is on the goods loop that runs from Totton to Fawley. Opened on 20 July 1925 as the Totton, Hythe (Hants) and Fawley (Hants) Light Railway, it formed the only connection between the oil refinery at Fawley and the outside world. Originally, the single track was worked by tablet and there was only one block controlled by Tyer's no. 7 electric train tablet instruments at Fawley and Eling (G.E.C. Webb, 'By light railway to Fawley', *The Railway Magazine* 94 (577), 307, Sept./Oct. 1948).

Construction of extensive sidings at Marchwood during the Second World War necessitated division of the line into two blocks. The no. 7 instrument at Eling was moved to Marchwood for the Marchwood–Fawley block and the block from Eling to Marchwood was worked with Tyer's no. 6 instruments.

The signal-box at Marchwood is an extension to the platform buildings. In the above photograph, taken looking towards Fawley, the signal-box can be seen jutting onto the platform. Diverging to the left is the line leading to Marchwood Military Port.

David Hucknall

Ash Vale station lies between Pirbright Junction and Farnham on the former LSWR line which was opened on 2 May 1870. Just beyond the station the line to Frimley and Ascot diverges from the Pirbright Junction line and follows the disused Basingstoke Canal towards Frimley. Ash Vale Junction 'box is located just after the junction by the side of the Frimley line. It is a non-standard LSWR 'box. It was opened in 1879, the year the Ash Vale–Frimley line opened. Significantly altered over the years (it has had individual function switches since 1971), the 'box looks clean and well-cared for, apart from the tagging.

December 1995 David Hucknall

The former LSWR Type 4 signal-box at Farnham. It stands on the Down side of the line, just west of Farnham station and just before the start of the single section to Alton.

The Type 4 'boxes were introduced in 1894/5 and the design was used until 1928. The one at Farnham dates from 1901 and shows many characteristic features. It is made of dark-coloured brick with a brick pillar interrupting the glazing. The window frames have gently curving tops and alternate sections slide to give access for cleaning.

Farnham signal-box has a Stevens' 1901 RSCo frame and an Entry–Exit panel which was fitted in 1985. It is on the Alton–Pirbright Junction section with the NX panel controlling Bentley and Alton stations.

August 1994 David Hucknall

Collingbourne station and signal-box were opened on 1 May 1882 by the Swindon, Marlborough and Andover Railway. Towards the end of the Down (Ludgershall-bound) platform sat the signal-box. It was small (14 ft by 12 ft) and built by the Gloucester Carriage and Wagon Company. Even in its heyday, it had only 16 levers, 2 of which were spare. Under the Midland and South Western Junction Railway (formed by amalgamation of the SMAR with the Swindon and Cheltenham Extension Railway), it was open from 8.00 a.m. to 6.30 p.m. on weekdays.

When the Western Region of British Railways re-acquired control of the line from the Southern Region in 1958, the line rapidly declined. By remodelling Lansdown Junction in Cheltenham to prevent connection with the Midland Region at Lansdown station, the major source of revenue for the route dried up. Eighty years after the opening of the SMAR, on 9 September 1961, all passenger and through goods services ended. The rapid decay and destruction of the stations and their 'boxes was inevitable.

H.G. Usmar/Author Collection

An undated photograph of the signal-box at Ludgershall on the former Midland and South Western Junction Railway. It was erected in 1901 by J.F. Pease and Co. The MSWJR was closely linked to the LSWR prior to the Grouping and Ludgershall signal-box had great similarity to that company's Type 4 design (compare Haslemere). Even the frame which was installed was that from the pre-1901 'box at Grateley.

H.G. Usmar/Author Collection

FORMER LBSCR LINES

LINES ALONG THE SOUTH COAST

The former London Brighton and South Coast Railway signal-box at Chichester is a handsome structure. It was opened in 1882 and built by Saxby and Farmer. Classified as a Saxby and Farmer Type 5, it lends weight to the opinion that this was 'one of the most stylish box designs ever built' (*The Signal-Box*, 1986, p. 81). Chichester's 'box has panelled brickwork and a hipped roof with a significant overhang. When this photograph was taken, its woodwork was painted in a striking light blue and white. It once overlooked the lines leading to and from the Up west sidings. It is typical of recent developments in Britain that it now overlooks a car park and a supermarket.

August 1994 David Hucknall

Barnham station (22 miles 29 chains from Brighton) lies on the section of the former LBSCR line between Ford Junction and Chichester. It also stands at the junction of the branch to Bognor Regis.

The signal-box at Barnham is large (probably the largest on the south coast) and stands at the west end of the Down platform. It controls the main line from Woodhorn level-crossing in the west to about ½ a mile east of Yapton level-crossing and the junction of the branch to Bognor Regis. Opened in 1911 by the LBSCR, the 'box is a Type 3b with a 75-lever frame. This photograph of part of the north elevation shows some of the large number of levers in this 'box.

On 1 August 1962, Barnham was the site of an unusual derailment. The accident occurred when the 10.17 a.m. from Brighton to Portsmouth left the rails because of half-open points on the approach to the station. The leading coach ran up the platform ramp before overturning onto the opposite track. Fortunately, casualties were not serious.

The points involved were motor-driven and controlled by a lever in Barnham signal-box some distance away. The lever was mechanically connected to a circuit controller, which was rotated by the lever movement to make or break contact as required. Examination of the point controller showed that a metal washer had become lodged in it in such a way that a complete circuit between the running rails, the reverse point operating wire, the point motor and earth was being made.

31 March 1996 David Hucknall

Part of the LBSCR 1905 Pattern signal frame inside Barnham signal-box. Many of the levers are out of use and painted white but operational in this view are no. 1, from Up main ground signal at points 7: no. 7, main crossover points no. 1: no. 8, Down main to loop points: no. 15, from Down main ground signal over points 7: no. 17, loop Up starting.

Some of the instruments on the block shelf are also visible.

David Hucknall

Signal levers inside the 'box at Barnham. Just visible on the left-hand side is no. 36 Up main starting.

The ubiquitous computer keyboard now adorns the instrument shelf. The winged armchair and the well-stocked book shelf will help the signalman to pass the time when rail traffic is light.

David Hucknall

The present signal-box at Bognor Regis is the third one to be erected since the station opened in June 1864. The first 'box was closed when a new station building came into use in 1902. Its place was taken by an 80-lever structure adjacent to the then engine shed.

The 'box shown in this photograph was opened in 1938. It is in the Southern Railways' 'Odeon' style. When this photograph was taken, considerable repairs were being carried out to the station-end following a collision. A 66-lever signal-box, it stands at the entrance to what had been the station yard and carriage sidings. The bridge in the background, behind the right-hand bracket signal, is the Bersted Crossing footbridge.

March 1996 David Hucknall

This photograph of Bognor Regis signal-box was taken in March 1996 during its reconstruction after it was hit by a train. Through the protective fencing details of the end elevation can be seen. The brickwork is embellished by two 'torches', apparently cast in cement, an interesting reflection on the style and attitude of the Southern Railway in the late 1930s.

David Hucknall

Havant signal-box stands on the Down side of the railway some 130 yds to the east of the station, overseeing a level-crossing. It is a pleasant-looking Saxby and Farmer Type 5 dating from 1876. Brick-built, with ivy beginning to spread over its walls, it has Saxby and Farmer's usual overhanging roof and eaves brackets. Its sliding windows retain the curved top frames which were also a feature of the Type 5 'boxes.

The 'box controls the line from Farlington Junction, 3 miles 323 yds to the west, to just beyond Emsworth station on the Brighton line. On the direct line, it now works with Petersfield 'box although, until their closure, there were additional 'boxes at Buriton Sidings, Idsworth Crossing and Rowland's Castle station. In this photograph, a train has just left platform 1 of the station and is about to swing to the left on to the Up main line.

August 1994 David Hucknall

The signal-box at Littlehampton. The 'box controls the lines in and around the station and as far as Littlehampton Junction where control is handed to Arundel.

The signal-box is a former LBSCR Type 2a. Characteristic features are the valancing (in the style of contemporary railway stations) and the hipped slate roof. Evidence of the existence of locking-room windows can also be clearly seen.

31 March 1996 David Hucknall

The signal-box at Pevensey and Westham is a delightful little structure on the line between St Leonards and Lewes. It stands at the west end of the Down platform. A Saxby and Farmer Type 5 'box built for the LBSCR and opened in 1876, it is fitted with the maker's Rocker-frame, having 14 levers. Standing on one of the small roads that run between Westham and Eastbourne, it oversees a level-crossing and controls the eastbound line up to a point midway between the Pevensey Sluice level-crossing and Cooden Beach.

14 June 1996 David Hucknall

The timber signal-box at Seaford began operating in 1895. It is a LBSCR Type 2c with 24 levers. By the time this photograph was taken, it was permanently switched out and the points in the station area had been clipped and padlocked for running into platform 2 only of the station. Once painted cream, the paint was badly flaking and being nagged by a strongly blowing wind from the sea. Just discernible through the windows are the handles of the levers and the instrument shelf. The three-aspect signal SF10 is at the end of the island platform and the now disused line to platform is in the foreground.

30 June 1996 David Hucknall

Berwick station is on the former LBSCR line between Lewes and St Leonards which opened on 27 June 1846. It is a small station with a level-crossing and signal-box at the eastern end of the platforms. At the end of the Down platform stands a home signal, the post of which was made, in thrifty Southern Railways' style, from old rails.

Berwick 'box is compact and well cared for; its windows shine. A Saxby and Farmer Type 5 of 1879, it controls approximately seven miles of route from Bedingham in the west to the level-crossing near Wilmington in the east.

14 June 1996 David Hucknall

It is difficult to imagine Newhaven as 'the Liverpool of the South with a dock extending as far as Lewes'. Nevertheless, these were the expectations five years after the opening of the branch from Southerham Junction, Lewes to Newhaven on 8 December 1847 (G.A. Sekon. 'The LBSCR East Coast Section - 2', *The Railway Magazine*, 93 (576), July/August 1948, p. 260). Newhaven never did develop to fulfil the expectations of the railway company.

This photograph shows the 1879 signal-box at Newhaven Town station (56.2 miles from London Bridge). A timber Saxby and Farmer Type 5 'box, built for the LBSCR, it was fitted with a Westinghouse A2 frame in 1953. The level-crossing overseen by the 'box is at a point where the old road between Brighton and Seaford crosses the railway. Any view of this box is dominated by the fly-over that carries the present A259. With a gesture that is so typical of the signalmen of Britain, window-boxes with a dazzling display of flowers had been attached to this dull and dirty 'box.

30 June 1996 David Hucknall

On 30 June 1862, the LBSCR obtained an act to extend the Lewes–Newhaven Harbour line to Seaford. This was opened on 1 June 1864.

Newhaven Harbour signal-box stands just over ¼ mile from Newhaven Harbour station. It overlooks the line down to Newhaven Marine station and the quay where refrigerated fruit-carrying ships still dock. The Seaford branch crossing of Beach Road is nearby.

Identified as a Saxby and Farmer Type 5 of 1886 (*The Signal-box Directory*, 1992), Newhaven Harbour 'box has changed considerably over the years. The two by two pane sections of the operating floor windows have lost their curved tops. The upper lights have been painted over and the locking-room windows have been bricked up. Watching an empty two-coach electric train trundle away towards Seaford, it was hard to believe that heavy boat expresses from Victoria once served Newhaven harbour.

David Hucknall

Dorking is on the line from Leatherhead to Horsham. The present signal-box at Dorking is located slightly beyond and behind the London end of the Down platform, 20 miles from Waterloo via Worcester Park. It is a Southern Railways Type 13, opened in 1938, with the eye-catching style that has been commented on elsewhere in this book. Although the original name remains in place, it is painted garishly in scarlet. At the end of the platform, three aspect signals CBK 38 and 39 can be seen.

David Hucknall

Twenty-seven miles from Waterloo via Worcester Park, Holmwood is on the line between Dorking and Horsham. Its signal-box, which stands approximately halfway along the Up platform, is yet another example of the delightful Type 5 design by Saxby and Farmer for the LBSCR. Dating from 1877, it has an 18-lever frame but is nowadays out of use.

It is gradually falling into disrepair. Its pleasant light blue and white paintwork is flaking while some of the upper lights are broken. The window at the Dorking end of the 'box is also boarded up.

30 June 1996 David Hucknall

Christ's Hospital station opened on 28 April 1902, specifically for the school which had moved from Newgate Street, London, to its present site in that year. The new station, known as Christ's Hospital, West Horsham, was built on the west side of Stammerham Junction in the middle of the Sussex countryside. Here, the cross-country route to Guildford, opened in 1865 by the LBSCR, diverged from the Horsham–Petworth line.

At the time of opening, the station was '. . . of neat design and harmonises well with the red brick of the adjacent school buildings' (H.A. Vallance, 'The Horsham-Guildford line', *The Railway Magazine*, 96 (593), Sept. 1950, p. 584). Passenger accommodation was generous, as befitted a junction of lines to Guildford, Shoreham and Pulborough, and to accommodate school specials.

Christ's Hospital station and its signal-box are sadly in decline. The 'box is now shabby with ugly additions and, behind it, there is now a wilderness of scrubby trees where the Guildford branch once diverged, initially as a double track. The buildings have been swept away, replaced by an absolute minimum of facilities on weed-covered platforms.

David Hucknall

Next to the racecourse, with the South Downs rising in the distance, the signal-box at Plumpton is delightfully situated. The former LBSCR Type 2b structure of 1891 (*The Signal-Box Directory*, 1992) harmonizes so well with its surroundings. It is painted dark cream and green, with an ivy-covered brick base and hipped slate roof. The most notable feature of the 'box is the large, finialled ventilator on the roof. Even the crossing gates are in the old style and do not intrude on the scene.

Plumpton station is on the Wivelsfield to Lewes line which was opened on 1 October 1847. Up trains travel to Croydon and London, Down trains to Lewes, Eastbourne and Hastings.

30 June 1996 David Hucknall

Amberley station is on the former LBSCR line from Horsham to Littlehampton which passes through Christ's Hospital, Billingshurst and Pulborough on its way to Arundel and Ford Junction. The route, having been built across undulating Wealden clays on its way to Pulborough, headed for the Arun gap in the South Downs. The descent into the Arun valley was blocked by a chalk projection at Amberley. Behind the station awning in the photograph, part of this obstacle can be seen. Amberley signal-box projects onto the Down platform. Opened in 1934, it has a 14-lever Stevens Knee (Tyer) frame. The 'box was deserted, used only to provide passengers with a sheltering wall from a cold wind.

March 1996 David Hucknall

Pulborough station is attractive. Its buildings are in a style which could be described as exaggerated Georgian. The signal-box stands slightly behind and toward the end of no. 1 platform. A Saxby and Farmer Type 5 'box of 1878, it seems to be in good condition. Apart from the modifications to the entrance (in the form of a lean-to porch and the ubiquitous 'Portaloo') it has many attractive, original features. The brick base is panelled and the locking-room windows are intact. The hipped roof with its small eaves brackets now painted light blue is typical and the upper lights between the roof and the main working floor windows have not been painted out. Some of the working-floor windows (two panes deep) have original curved tops to the frames.

31 March 1996 David Hucknall

Arundel is on the Pulborough to Ford Junction section of the former LBSCR line opened on 3 August 1863. The station (approximately 58 miles from London Bridge via Redhill) lies about 1 mile from the town in a shallow cutting on flat ground close to the River Arun.

The signal-box stands a short distance from the station on the down Horsham side. Opened in 1938, it is a former Southern Railway Type 13 'box fitted with an 'NX' panel in 1979. With deep, plain windows with solid-looking frames on the working level, an overhanging flat roof and its name in large, clear letters, Arundel signal-box typifies the confident style of Southern Railway architecture in the 1930s.

David Hucknall

FORMER SECR LINE

Bopeep Junction is approximately 1¾ miles from Hastings station at the western entrance to Bopeep Tunnel (1,318 yds long). It was always an important frontier on the railway network of the south coast of England. In pre-Grouping days, it marked the point of convergence of the LBSCR route from Lewes to St Leonards and the SER line from Battle to St Leonards and Hastings. Although the SER owned the line through Warrior Square station to Hastings, the LBSCR had running powers from Bopeep Junction into Hastings. The signal-box at Bopeep Junction is seen here from platform 2 of West St Leonards station. The 'box was opened by the SER in about 1887, although the present frame is reconditioned and was fitted by Westinghouse in 1973.

According to *The Railway Magazine* (R.A.H. Weight, July 1940), the name 'Bopeep' was taken from a local public house. That had been sited in an area which the article claims was 'the haunt of shepherds who are sometimes reputed to have lost their sheep on the adjacent marshes'.

14 June 1996 David Hucknall

SCOTTISH REGION

After nationalization, the Scottish Region of British Railways was responsible for the two divisions (the LMS and the LNER) that had administered traffic control and signalling for some twenty-five years. In Scotland, the constituent companies of the LNER included the North British and the Great North of Scotland Railway Companies, while the LMS consisted of the Caledonian Railway, the Glasgow and South Western Railway and the Highland Railway. It is remarkable that, at the end of the twentieth century, through the signalling system, so many reminders of the pre-Grouping days in Scotland remain.

This chapter is concerned predominantly with the route from Glasgow to Aberdeen via Perth. Even then, it is quite restricted. Only one former GNSR 'box (Ballater) is shown and the Highland Railway is similarly represented by one of the 'boxes at Inverness. The GSWR is not discussed.

Power signalling came relatively early to Scotland. In 1908, the signalling at Glasgow Central was modernized to bring the entire section under the control of one 'box. The frame was built by the McKenzie, Holland and Westinghouse Power Signal Company. It had 374 miniature levers. Similarly, enlargement of St Enoch station brought about the installation of a system whereby points were actuated mechanically, but signals were operated electrically. By 1931, the St Enoch system had been replaced by a power installation and a colour-light system. After nationalization, further progress was made. The use of track circuitry and colour lights allowed replacement of groups of small signal-boxes by larger central 'boxes. The 'box at Cowlains, opened in 1956, was a good example of this. It replaced eight signal-boxes which had, up to then, controlled a complex arrangement of junctions. Glasgow Central power 'box, opened in 1961, replaced the original power 'box mentioned earlier and two mechanical 'boxes which had been located at Bridge Street Junction and Eglinton Street. When it opened, the later 'box had the capacity to set more than 1,000 routes to deal with the actual and predicted density of rail traffic.

In spite of such early and significant advances, the AB method of manual signalling still remains in use in Scotland. Apart from its former GSWR routes between Ayr and Stranraer and Annan and Kilmarnock, an extensively manually-signalled route is that between Glasgow, Queen Street and Aberdeen via Perth. Prior to the closure of Buchanan St station in November 1966, Glasgow–Aberdeen trains ran via Cumbernauld. The line from Gartsherrie to Greenhill that passes through Cumbernauld remains AB-signalled as far as Cumbernauld but it is then TCB-signalled to Carmuirs West Junction. From Carmuirs West Junction to Perth, there is an extensive stretch of AB signalling through Larbert, Stirling, Dunblane, Auchterarder to Hilton Junction. At Larbert, the line is joined by another AB-signalled route, that from Grangemouth and Falkirk. 'Traditional' 'boxes exist at Fouldubs Junction, Grangemouth

Junction, Swing Bridge East and Carmuirs East Junction. It is interesting to note that the AB section between the Middle and North 'boxes at Stirling, at 660 yards, is one of the shortest in the country.

Another extensive AB-signalled section lies between Dundee and Aberdeen. It extends from Carnoustie to Newtonhill, apart from a section between Usan and Montrose South. On this route, the 'boxes originate either with the Caledonian or North British Railways. They include Stonehaven (CR, 1901), Carmont (CR, *c.* 1876), Laurencekirk (CR, 1901), Craigo (CR, *c.* 1881), Ulsan (NBR, 1906), Inverkeilor (NBR, 1881) and Arbroath (NBR, 1911).

The NBR and CR signal-boxes are invariably brick-built and generally in a reasonable condition structurally. Both companies tended to favour hipped roof designs. The Caledonian Railways from the 1890s used contractors to build 'boxes to the railway's own design. It differentiated between Northern and Southern divisions. The majority of former CR 'boxes shown in this chapter are Northern division Type 2 designs.

In Scotland, the LMS and LNER both used the upper quadrant type of semaphore signal to replace the lower quadrant signals of the pre-Grouping companies. The most characteristic feature was on the North British semaphores. They had 'pear-shaped' spectacle glasses which were the speciality of the signalling contractor Stevens and Sons. Arms on the Caledonian Railway signals had adjustable spectacles. Although in a location such as Stirling it is common to find standard upper quadrant arms on pre-Grouping signal posts, one will be very, very unlikely to encounter a genuine pre-Grouping signal. Even on remote branches in England, they had probably disappeared by the 1980s. Nevertheless, at Stirling station, there remains a genuine rarity – a Caledonian Railway lower quadrant signal.

This view shows Stirling station looking towards Stirling Middle signal-box. In spite of losing a magnificent signal gantry, Stirling retains a superb array of semaphore signals.

Stirling station was opened in 1848 by the Scottish Central Railway although the present buildings date from 1915. It always had principal and subsidiary platforms, dating from pre-nationalization days when the LMSR owned and staffed the station and the LNER used the spartan easternmost side.

Stirling station remains a pleasure to visit. The former LMSR platforms are spotlessly clean and the station lighting has been thoughtfully and sympathetically chosen.

28 August 1996 David Hucknall

A fascinating signal at Stirling station. The left-hand bracket, double lattice-post signal has both upper and lower quadrant arms (signals no. 17 and 14, respectively, on the Stirling Middle signal-box diagram). Signal 14 is the last working lower quadrant arm on Railtrack Scotland. This photograph also shows clearly the Stevens' 'open ball' finials on the tops of the posts. This design of finials was used by the North British Railway (and the GN of SR).

The standard one-arm ground signal (no. 12) which can be seen is also elevated on a lattice post. All three signals stand close to the now-disused car carrier lye.

28 August 1996 David Hucknall

In this photograph, published before but showing nevertheless the size of Stirling Middle signal-box superbly, class A2 4–6–2 no. 60527 *Sun Chariot* is seen roaring past the 'box with the 1.30 p.m. Aberdeen to Glasgow train. The date is 8 June 1963. Just 138 yards further on was a fine signal gantry that carried eleven semaphore signals.

Both Stirling Middle and North signal-boxes survive as examples of the Caledonian Railway's Type N2 (N for Northern division) structures. In spite of the fact that the gantry has now gone, demolished in February 1985, Stirling still has a marvellous variety of semaphore signals, including a survivor from the Caledonian Railway.

W.A.C. Smith

Kingmoor 'Jubilee' class 4–6–0s, no. 45728 *Defiance* and no. 45718 *Dreadnought* leave Perth station with the 12.10 p.m. train to Euston. Some of the semaphore signals that permitted movements at the south end of the station can be seen in front of the overall station roof. The main platforms of the station were signalled for Up and Down running and controlled by two 'boxes. One, the Down Centre Box, had 20 levers and controlled the north ends of the platforms. The Up Centre Box (41 levers) controlled activities at the south end of the platforms as well as movements to and from the carriage sheds.

Before the opening of the power signal-box at Perth in 1962, some ten mechanical signal-boxes controlled about 2 miles of track, from Friarton in the south to Balhousie in the north, with Perth station situated approximately midway. In addition to those mentioned, these included Friarton and the 'boxes at Edinburgh Road, St Leonards Bridge, St Leonards Junction, Glasgow Road, Dovecoteland Junction and Balhousie. The tenth 'box was Orchardbank, a small, 15-lever structure at the east end of the Dundee platforms.

28 May 1960 W.A.C. Smith

(*Opposite, bottom*) Perth is approached from the south through Moncrieff Tunnel. Hilton Junction (2⅛ miles south of Perth), is separated from the tunnel entrance by a short, steep, rocky cutting.

At the junction, the lines from Glasgow via Stirling and Edinburgh converge. In this photograph, the former Caledonian Railway Type N1 signal-box of 1873 at Hilton Junction can be seen. Approaching the junction is A4 class 4–6–2 no. 60012 *Commonwealth of Australia* with the 10.30 a.m. Edinburgh–Perth train.

Hilton Junction signal-box survived the opening of the new Perth 'box in 1962 and the latter is the next in the down direction. Both survive today.

W.A.C. Smith

Details of the ex-Caledonian Railway signal-box at Larbert North are shown here as a train passes by in front. The paintwork is flaking and the putty on the window frames is crumbling. Outside, a couple of mops are drying.

29 August 1996 David Hucknall

Passing the signal-box at Larbert North is the 10.00 a.m. Euston to Perth train, pulled by 'Royal Scot' class 4–6–0 no. 46160 *Queen Victoria's Rifleman*. The signal-box, a Northern Division, former Caledonian Railway Type 2 of 1892, is still in use. Although the semaphore signals outside the 'box have been removed, several examples remain.

Larbert station (8 miles from Stirling) is on a slightly rising (1 in 253) section of the line. Shortly after the station, however, the gradient falls at 1 in 163 towards the site of the former Alloa Junction, before rising again at 1 in 126 for two miles to Plean Junction.

Since this photograph was taken, Larbert station has been altered considerably. The original buildings have been swept away, replaced by probably much more comfortable glass and steel structures. On the wall of the Up platform, however, there is a marble plaque which stands as a reminder of events long past. It commemorates the men of the 1st/7th Royal Scots, Leith Territorial Division. In 1915, they left Larbert station to serve in the First World War, only to be killed in the disaster near the signal-box at Quintinshill, between Gretna and Kirkpatrick: 227 people died and 250 were injured. All but twelve of the dead were men of the Royal Scots.

31 July 1963 W.A.C. Smith

The former Caledonian Railway signal-box at Larbert Junction. This photograph makes an interesting contrast with Bill Smith's shot of the same 'box taken some thirty-three years earlier. The original name, 'Larbert Jct', has been removed but the board remains, the locking-room windows are now bricked up and the top of the chimney is missing. Unusually, however, the balcony outside the windows now has guard rails. The pole at the corner of the 'box remains.

Not knowing the area particularly well, I found the signal-box with difficulty. It is approached through the yard of a small engineering company which is reached via an unmade road that runs hard against the railway viaduct. This carries the railway across the A9 between Larbert and Camelon.

David Hucknall

Polmont shed's J37 class 0–6–0 no. 64537 passes the signal-box at Larbert Junction (abbreviated as 'Junct' on the nameboard) heading towards Larbert with a down freight on 12 September 1963. Larbert Junction is on a triangular arrangement of lines. Diverging to the left in this photograph can be seen the line to Falkirk via Carmuirs East Junction, built by the Stirlingshire Midland Junction Company. The line on which the J37 is travelling comes via Carmuirs West Junction, from the south-west either from Cumbernauld or the Edinburgh and Glasgow route.

W.A.C. Smith

NORTH BRITISH RAILWAY

The construction by the North British Railway of the railway line between Montrose and Arbroath occurred relatively late in the nineteenth century. It was opened to passenger traffic from 1 March 1881. Montrose North signal-box dates from the opening. Built by Stevens for the NBR, it is classified as a Type 1 'box.

Passing Montrose North as it approaches the station, V2 class 2–6–0 no. 60956 is heading the 3.40 p.m. Aberdeen to Edinburgh Waverley. On the right-hand side of the locomotive is a siding; the miniature semaphore signals bracketed from the main post, and the ground disc signal, control movement to and from the sidings.

4 July 1959 W.A.C. Smith

(*Opposite, bottom*) Gartcosh Junction signal-box is one of three that control a triangular arrangement of former Caledonian Railway lines to the north of Coatbridge. South of Gartcosh, the lines lead to Coatbridge and Motherwell, to the south-west, to Springburn and Glasgow while to the north-east the lines pass through Cumbernauld and on to Larbert.

A former Caledonian Railway Type S4 'box of 1899, Gartcosh Junction is a sturdy brick-built structure. In this photograph, 'Black 5' class 4–6–0 no. 44677 passes the signal-box on the Up main line heading for Gartsherrie South Junction signal-box.

August 1966 W.A.C. Smith

GREAT NORTH OF SCOTLAND RAILWAY

Ballater station was opened on 17 October 1866 by Aboyne and Braemar Railway Company. Progress in building the railway over the 43¼ miles from Aberdeen had been painfully slow. Proposals for the Deeside railway had been made in 1845 and authorization for a line from Ferryhill to Aboyne was given in July 1846. A line to Banchory was opened in December 1859 but completion of the section to Ballater was not achieved until 1866.

The station closed on 28 February 1966 and this photograph was taken in 1965. It shows lattice-post signals which once would have been lower quadrant at Ballater looking towards Cambus O'May. Ballater signal-box can be seen in the distance. It was a Great North of Scotland Railway Type 2 'box – plain, made of timber and with no adornment.

David Hucknall

This photograph, taken from the end of no. 3 platform at Inverness station, shows an Up train to Glasgow waiting at no. 2 platform, headed by a pair of Birmingham RCW Type '3' diesel-electric locomotives.

To the left of the leading locomotive is the former Highland Railway Loco Signal Cabin and further to the left is part of the Mechanical Engineer's Workshop, previously the HR's Lochgorm Works. Apart from the loco signal cabin, other signal-boxes in the vicinity of Inverness station were Millburn Junction, Welsh's Bridge and Rose St Bridge Junction; the approach to the station from the south and east was controlled by Millburn Junction 'box and Welsh's Bridge 'box.

April 1965 David Hucknall

ACKNOWLEDGEMENTS

It gives me very great pleasure to acknowledge the help and assistance given to me in the preparation of this book. My particular thanks go to Mrs Renate McCarron who typed the manuscript with such efficiency and accuracy.

I should like to express my sincere appreciation to David Holmes, Lawrence James, Howard Lorriman, Nigel Mussett and Bill Smith who made some of their superb photographs available to me. My thanks are also due to Peter Alvey who allowed me to use some of his late uncle's fascinating pictures and to Dudley Jones who made his extensive library of railway books and magazines always available. My special thanks to my niece Sarah Turvey who spent part of an Easter holiday photographing Abergele and Rhyl for me.

I am also indebted to all the railway personnel who have assisted me in obtaining material for this book. Thanks are particularly due to Brian Bates, Signalling Manager, Railtrack, at Worksop and Keith Bowden, Manager, South West Trains Bournemouth Traction and Rolling Stock Maintenance Depot.

Finally, it goes without saying that without the considerable help of my wife Susan and my children Rachel and Philip, it would have been exceedingly difficult to obtain the photographs in this book. They have been prepared to tolerate some extraordinary detours as we have travelled up and down the country.

BIBLIOGRAPHY

Allen, D. and Wolstenholmes, C.J. *A Pictorial Survey of Railway Signalling*, Oxford Publishing Co., Sparkford, 1991

——*A Pictorial Survey of London–Midland Signalling*, OPC, Sparkford, 1996

Anderson, P. *Railways of Lincolnshire*, P. Anderson/Irwell Press, 1992

Bairstow, M. *The Huddersfield and Sheffield Junction Railway*, M. Bairstow, Halifax, 1993

——*Railways in East Yorkshire*, vol. 2, Amadeus Press, 1995

Bairstow, M. and Beeker, D. *Railways around Harrogate*, vol. 2, Allenwood Press Ltd, Pudsey, 1988

Batty, S.R. *Rail Centres: Doncaster*, Ian Allen, London, 1991

Behrend, G. *'Don't Knock the Southern'*, Midland Publishing Co., Leicester, 1993

Bennett, A. *Southern Holiday Lines in North Cornwall and West Devon*, Runpast Publications, 1995

——*Great Western Railway in West Cornwall*, Kingfisher Railway Productions, Southampton, 1988

Binns, D. *'Little' North-Western Railway, Skipton North Junction–Lancaster and the Ingleton–Low Gill Branch*, vol. 1, Channel View Publications, Clevedon, 1994

Body, G. *'Railways of the Eastern Region'*, *PSL Field Guide*, vol. 1, Patrick Stevens Ltd, 1989

Butt, R.V.J. *The Directory of Railway Stations*, PSL, 1995

Currey, J.H. *Block Instruments (British Practice) no. 12*, The Institution of Railway Signal Engineers, 1952

Dow, G. *Midland Style*, Historical Model Railway Society, 1975

Dyckhoff, N. *The Cheshire Lines Committee – Then and Now*, Ian Allen, 1984

Fawcett, R. *Ganger, Guard and Signalman*, Bradford Barton, Truro, 1981

Fiennes, G.F. *I tried to run a railway*, Ian Allan, Shepperton, 1967

Foster, R.D. *A Pictorial Record of LNWR Signalling*, Oxford Publishing Co., Oxford, 1982

Goode, C.T. *The Wakefield, Pontefract and Goole Railway*, CT. Goode, Hull, 1993

Gordon, D.I. *A Regional History of the Railways of Great Britain*, vol. 5, The Eastern Counties, 3rd edn, David St John Thomas/David and Charles, Newton Abbott, 1990

Hendry, R. Preston and Hendry, R. Powell. *An Historical Survey of Selected LMS Stations*, vol. 1, OPC, Poole, 1982

Hoole, K. *North-Eastern Branch Line Termini*, Oxford Publishing Co., Poole, 1985

Hurst, G. *LNWR Branch Lines of West Leicestershire and East Warwickshire*, Milepost Publications, Worksop, 1993

Jenkins, S.C. *The Wensleydale Branch – A New History*, The Oakwood Press, 1993

Jordan, S. *The Bognor Branch Line*, The Oakwood Press, Oxford, 1989

Kay, P./The Signalling Study Group. *The Signal-Box Directory, 1992*, P. Kay, Teignmouth, 1992

——*Signalling Atlas and Signal-Box Directory*, P. Kay, Teignmouth, 1997

Kichenside, G.M. and Williams, A. *British Railway Signalling*, 4th edn, Ian Allan, London, 1978

MacClean, A.A. *A Pictorial Record of LNER Constituent Signalling*, OPC, Oxford, 1983

Mitchell, V. and Smith, K. *Southern Main Lines: Crawley to Littlehampton*, Middleton Press, 1986

——*Southern Main Lines: Bournemouth to Weymouth*, Middleton Press, Midhurst, 1988

Pearson, M. *Pearson's Railway Rides: Cotswolds and Malverns*, J.M. Pearson and Sons, 1994

Potts, C.R. *An Historical Survey of Selected GW Stations*, vol. 2, Oxford Publishing Co., Sparkford, 1988

——*An Historical Survey of Selected GW Stations*, vol. 4, Oxford Publishing Co., Poole, 1985

Pryer, G.A. *Signal-Box Diagrams of the Great Western and Southern Railways*, vol. 2, *SR Lines in East Dorset*, G.A. Pryer, Southampton

Signalling Study Group, *The Signal-Box: A Pictorial History and Guide to Designs*, Oxford Publishing Co., Poole, 1986

Vaughan, A. *A Pictorial Record of Great Western Signalling*, Oxford Publishing Co., Oxford, 1973

——*Signalman's Reflections*, Silver Link Publishing, 1991

Warburton, L.G. and Anderson, V.R. *A Pictorial Record of LMS Signals*, Oxford Publishing Co., Oxford, 1972

Yonge, J. *Track Diagrams – England South and London Underground*, ed. G. Jacobs, Quail Map Co., Exeter, 1994

——*Track Diagrams 4. London Midland Region*, ed. G. Jacobs, Quail Map Co., 1990

INDEX

INDEX